Iconoclasm

Political Empowerment for the New Millennium

By Jaron D. Pearlman

iconoclasm: *The action of attacking or assertively challenging beliefs and institutions or established values and practices*

Foreword

I have always heard that experience is the best teacher. Experience provides insight, context, examples, and individual ideas for every subject; through experience we don't just learn peripherally, we learn directly. Throughout my life I have admired those with wide experience in different subjects, or those who have simply had unique experiences in their lives. That's the great thing about it: no two experiences are the same. Perhaps comparable, but never the same. Each individual has a personally woven design made just for them. In having this we are all able to communicate and share what we experience, enlarging and supplementing the experiences of others. I think that's why I enjoy traveling so much—you never know who you may meet and what they have to show you.

I spent many years on the road meeting people, but it wouldn't be until I became a teacher that I would recollect an experience from my childhood that made me decide to write this book.

I was a science teacher and my class was learning about biology. In an unusual class discussion we began to talk about social hierarchy in mammals, which naturally led to how human beings have arranged our own social concepts. I described a variety of social structures, such as feudalism, castes, monarchies, and democracies. As I am sure at this point I was rambling, one of the smartest girls in the class decided to rattle my chain by saying: "Why can't we all just live off the grid? This is all too complicated. We should just look out for ourselves."

I answered her by explaining that humans were more efficient in groups, but her question made me remember something else.

Though she was clearly joking, I remember having that same question during a classroom election in grade school.

When I was in second grade we learned about democracy. Granted, with young kids there is only so much you can really teach—the basic concept of the democratic process is within their understanding, but not something like the Electoral College System. I remember at that time there was a presidential election between Bill Clinton and George H. W. Bush. We set up ballot boxes in the classroom and we were to go home and ask our parents about the election, casting our own votes the next day.

We were so young I imagine a lot of what our parents told us regarding the candidate platforms went right over our heads. The classroom ballots that would be collected were almost certainly what our parents had told us to vote. Yet for the purpose of the project, we were meant to obtain a formative understanding of what it would mean to be a citizen in a democratic society. More to the point, what does it mean to be involved in civilization as a whole?

I cast my vote for the outlier, Ross Perot, a protest vote, if you will. Neither Clinton nor Bush was appealing to my family, for reasons I didn't yet understand. I went to class that day and found there was no ballot box for my candidate. Only Bush and Clinton had collection boxes, and I was the only kid asking for another option. I approached my teacher and questioned why there was no mention of the other options, or even a box for the person my family had directed me toward.

"Well, he has no chance of winning. You're the only one that even knows who he is. Just pick one of the other two so we can count the ballots and you won't be left out."

I am paraphrasing (this was a long time ago) but the last bit I remember very clearly:

". . . and you won't be left out."

Even though I didn't know who these candidates were, what they stood for, or how politics worked, I felt more left out because I couldn't use my vote the way I wanted to. It made me wonder why we even held the election. Why even be part of the class democracy?

I don't bring this up with the intention of dissecting the efficacy of protest votes. I bring it up because it is the first time I remember questioning the purpose of a society in my youth. Voting for a leader isn't a luxury that many nations have. Even in the recent past, democratic participation has only extended to a small margin of the populace.

What I took out of that classroom experiment was not an understanding of how democracy worked; rather it was how democracy had failed to work.

Majority-ruled decisions would continue to pique my curiosity over the years. If people didn't have the information they needed in order to make a decision, how could they make good decisions? It would appear increasingly as I grew older that neither riches, nor democracy, nor partisan politics equated to freedom.

Only information equates to freedom.

The following is meant to be a dialogue, wide in range and for the purposes of assessing the natural priority of society. It is meant to categorize and analyze various elements, structures, and actions between a government and its people, as well as address the ever-growing paradigm of globalized exchange. Even a little over two decades ago the world was so different than it is now, and yet it is very much the same. The purpose of society has never truly changed, even throughout all its radical incarnations.

Social living is meant to provide a better quality of life to more people. It is meant to help us share our experiences.

Many civil experiments aimed to these ends have proven very unsuccessful. Many have also been manipulated into perverse doppelgangers of their initial intent. It is my opinion that within the seminal effort to unify, civilized growth can still be realized. It is in that effort that we do not have to agree, we do not have to even love each other. It is in that effort that we can recognize that strength lies in informed differences and knowledgeable discussion.

I have little doubt in my mind that information is the means to societal and political evolution. I also have little doubt that said information must be obtained through some widened context, which I have done my best to provide with as little conjecture as possible. Each section of this book is written with the intention to alleviate the confusion that surrounds affairs both macro and micro, domestic and foreign, practical and moral. It is my sincere hope that the following aids in the concern that I think many of us share:

That we are not left out.

jp

Table of Contents

Foundations

The human being is in the most literal sense a political animal, not merely a gregarious animal, but an animal which can individuate itself only in the midst of a society.
—Karl Marx

Society has always to demand a little more from human beings than it will get in practice.
—George Orwell

I know of no safe depository of the ultimate powers of the society but the people themselves; and if we think them not enlightened enough to exercise their control with a wholesome discretion, the remedy is not to take it from them but to inform their discretion.
—Thomas Jefferson

In one of his opus literatures Francis Fukuyama states that human interaction, and thus societal development, often rests upon a pair of integral facets. Kin selection and reciprocal altruism both affect humanity as a cognitive bias, altering our social realities and making us favor those who we are related to biologically or those who have acted toward us favorably in the past.

Mr. Fukuyama presents the idea that even in the grand schemes of societal development, politics, and economics, the democratic world is perhaps smaller than we think. Due to aristocratic kin selection and reciprocal altruism, power has been consolidated time and time again from a historical standpoint.

For a social species, this is troubling. The irony couldn't be more devious; a creature that requires society both biologically and psychologically is undermined by the inherent conditions of its immediate social ties. Thus large-scale society seems to be a heinous catch-22: the quality of life is meant to be better for more people in a society, yet leadership roles are prone to create intense class divide as a result of kin selection and reciprocal altruism.

Considering all of this, what is the purpose of civilization?

There is one overall idea behind human beings joining together socially: to raise the quality of life for the majority. No matter the brand of leadership, political structure, or economic choices, banding together has brought humankind to the top of the food chain as the dominant species of Earth. By increasing our numbers and working together, jobs could be delegated, agriculture and technology could be created, security could be monitored, lifespans could be elongated. Society is a reflection of humanity, and humanity a reflection of society.

All structures of government and power have essentially been experiments in refining the above-stated goals. The complicity of a society's people toward social exchange is a recognition of the need for others. This need exists in order to establish four prominent foundations of civilization.

Liquidity

Imagine for a moment that you are a tailor, living in a village with a fisherman, a builder, and a cobbler. You will trade clothes with your fellow villagers for fish, shoes, or home repairs.

However, there is a significant problem:

Many nights you go hungry with no fish to eat, as the local fisherman does not need new clothes every day. You have nothing else to trade and little time to acquire new skills for your own benefit. Your home has holes in the roof, as the builder's trade costs are much higher than the worth of your clothing inventory. One of your shoes is repaired while the other is missing a sole, until the cobbler needs a new item from your stock.

The barter (trade) system frequently had missed connections like these, putting many people in compromising positions. The only functional equivalent to bartering was economic egalitarianism, where all goods and services were free and could be taken or administered as needed. This had its own limitations, becoming cumbersome and easily abused in anything larger than small tribal societies. The constraints that existed in a barter-based society became one of the first things to undermine large-scale societal progress. Populations grew under formative barter systems, but many individuals were unhealthy and in need of basic goods and services.

A form of liquidity was needed, meaning a medium through which all economic exchange could operate. A liquid asset could change the entire paradigm of the little village, allowing you to purchase fish even when the fisherman needed no clothes, fix your roof, get your matching shoe, and so on. Thus, with liquidity, your assets have diversified. You are able to sell clothes and purchase necessities based on your needs.

Put simply, this is all money is. Currency as a whole serves a singular purpose: liquidity.

The concept of liquid exchange is ancient. Initially, common resources that had a universal use were preferred. For example, obsidian was used as early as 15,000 BCE as a liquid medium. It was particularly in demand because of its use in stone tools; in cases like this, the choice of liquid assets had a practical purpose as well as an exchange-based use.

Examining monies from around the ancient globe reveals uses of other stones, shells, livestock, grains, beads, leaves, precious metals, guano, pelts, and much more.

Liquid wealth became more than a means of access to goods or services; it enabled a shift in the way societies would function. Power could be dispersed widely and nations could become larger, laying the framework for modern societies. Prior to the use of a liquid economic medium, social power was heavily consolidated by kin selection. Granted, many later societies would still face this issue, but the prospect of liquidity created a new type of power to be had: that of economic aptitude.

The idea of power was now not limited to that of lineage or control of labor, but could be exercised by those who accumulated liquid assets. Suddenly a person who did well in their trade could facilitate loans or purchases for those in need, acquire more resources than their peers, and ultimately generate power that had been unprecedented in tribal groups.

This concept deconsolidated previous kin relationship hierarchies, permanently changing the social incarnations to follow.

As the civilized world grew, liquid exchange became even more important. Just as in our village, Nation A that required imports could now purchase them from Nation B, even if B needed no actual goods from its client. If restricted by barter, Nation B would have no fair motivation to trade with a country that had nothing in demand. This principle allowed global commerce to make the nations of the world much larger and integrate products from all over the known earth, allowing the quality of life for human beings to improve overall.

This concept of liquidity, like many other inventions, has two sides to it. It would be unrealistic to view a liquid market as solely beneficial; the rise of currencies has also created much dismay. One can easily observe that the use of liquid monies has diversified the roster of social power, but it also allows for kin selection and reciprocal altruism.

A classic example of this would be corporate lobbyists paying a congressman to pass legislation that benefits their company. The underlying form of such reciprocity can hardly be called altruistic.

The idea of debt had been around during times of barter, yet was largely reined in by the tangible nature of trade-based exchange. For instance, going into debt over the things one needs (food, shelter, water, clothing) was far more common under a barter system, as debt resolution and interest accumulation were often definite. It wasn't as common to obtain things that weren't a necessity, partially because of the smaller nature of societies at the time and the limited range of products in the economic ecosystem. Going into debt due to extraneous purchases was of little or no possibility.

A drawback to the creation of a liquid market is the predatory nature of those who could lend, sell, or launder. The prospect of credit would become a massive business that could lend to more and more people, often for goods and services that were not as necessary as had been previously available in the system of barter.

Various terms, rates, and financial ideas could be created by those with the most liquidity at their disposal, for the purpose of homogenizing their ring of power and wealth. The idea of an economic aristocracy creating the rules for liquid exchange is akin to letting foxes run a henhouse.

Another jarring potential related to liquid exchange is the monopolization of currency. A liquid market works most efficiently under a specific pretense: that a multitude of currencies are in existence.

Consider one of the quintessential ideas behind money: it is a way to open up avenues of power and self-determination to more people. Should there be one determined currency, the entity behind said currency's creation or distribution would have a vastly unfair advantage over its economic participants. By diversifying the market of currencies, a plethora of nations can naturally check and balance each other in the grand scheme of wealth and power.

Professor David Graeber has some enlightening views on this detailed in his books *Debt: The First 5,000 Years* and *Essays on Hierarchy, Rebellion, and Desire* (2011). Among his musings are the idea that debt is an inherent human condition, from the debt to one's mother and father, to the moral debt placed at the helm of religious studies or political action, to the debt placed upon each other to coexist on this planet. Take for instance this wonderful quote detailing a relationship between expectation, fantasy, and liquidity:

*Traditional hedonism . . . was based on the direct
experience of pleasure: wine, women, and song; sex,
drugs, and rock and roll; or whatever the local variant.
The problem, from a capitalist perspective, is that there
are inherent limits to all this. People become sated,
bored. Modern self-illusory hedonism solves this
dilemma because here, what one is really consuming
are fantasies and daydreams about what having a
certain product WOULD be like.*

Another reads:

*If history shows anything, it's that there is no better
way to justify relations founded on violence, to make
such relations seem moral, than by reframing them in
the language of debt—above all, because it immediately
makes it seem that it's the victim that's doing something
wrong.*

Graeber examines the effects of liquid exchange and debt not only in the scope of trade and finance, but also from the perspective of the human condition. As with modernized democracy, a series of checks and balances must exist to even out the prospects of homogenization or monopoly from the use of currency.

As the world became more and more interconnected the exchange of liquid assets began to shape their respective countries. Based on the performance, currency base, and gross domestic product of Nation A, its coinage may be worth half of that from Nation B. This would mean for A to purchase products from B it would require twice the normal worth. Such exchange rates have determined the hierarchy of many civilizations throughout the world.

The competition involved between currencies likely improved national output from ancient civilizations, helping successful economic models thrive and allowing benign ones to fail. In essence, competing forms of currency were a type of global capitalism far before the rise of modern capitalism, prodding along an eat-or-be-eaten rhetoric of business.

While the factors in determining the international worth of currency are widely varied, one of the most important is that of a base. A *monetary base* refers to a settled upon substance to which money can be linked. Rephrasing, this would imply that a money made of paper or cloth could be directly redeemable to something desirable on the international market; gold, silver, or other precious metals have been widely popular. While the worth of a single unit of currency may fluctuate from a bar of gold to a half bar to an ounce or a gram, it still remained that no matter the international value of Nation A's money, a citizen could consider their liquid assets a symbolic method of exchange internationally.

Given that precious metals are in demand regardless of nationality, a redeemable currency base is an incredibly safe way to assure the intrinsic value of money. Should there be no base for Nation A's money, it would be only worth the paper or cloth the note was printed upon.

Basing currency also acts as a control upon currency inflation. Currency inflation often occurs when a nation mints or prints too much money, making it too common in the world marketplace and thereby decreasing its value. Counterintuitively, creating more money actually lowers its worth.

When based upon a physical holding of some kind (such as a precious metal), monetary inflation is held to a limit; that limit being the smallest amount of gold or silver marketable internationally. Without basing currency, money becomes elastic. Elastic currencies run the risk of being printed to the point they lose all purchasing power, leading to economic depression and collapse. Famous realities linked to inflationary fallout include the Weimar Republic (and subsequent Third Reich), the Roman Empire, and the Byzantine.

It is worth noting that as global societies progressed, mediums of liquid exchange became more and more abstract.

With bartering, all exchanges were based on necessity and tangibility. A good or service was needed, or at the very least was directly seen or understood. Food, shelter, and clothing are far from abstract; such commodities have definite and obvious value. Many of the first currencies were symbolic to an extent, but also had a practical purpose, whether it be for fashioning tools or for eating. Several economic generations later, common mediums were desired for their relative rarity. Coinage and rare precious stones may have been less useful than obsidian, but had vast pull in the market. Departing from coins would come paper or cloth notes which were more or less useless, but meant to symbolize a based physical holding of something desirable.

Tangibility became even farther removed with the ideas of investment exchange, stocks, bonds, put options, etc. Options became available to purchase shares of public or private endeavors, giving an entirely new level to the symbolic exchange of wealth and liquidity. These new methods would vary between *static exchange*, where investments have a guaranteed return, and *variable exchange*, where investments are equivalent to placing an economic bet. The murkier the waters of liquidity become, the more myriad the ways one may take advantage of others, or conversely, find their own unique market ingenuity.

Liquid exchange methods diversified along with social growth, accompanied by the expanding world of goods and services. The needs of the global market demanded more and more from concepts regarding liquid exchange, putting into motion countless experiments of both success and failure. While the initial purpose of liquidity is altruistic and undeniable, it can be easily manipulated without a system of checks and balances.

At its core the need for liquidity comes down to diversifying exchange, and thereby diversifying power. Liquid economics are meant to expand the ideas of individualism, life quality, and progress; yet this is not always the reality. For a society to progress and not become stagnant it must actively monitor the state of its liquidity.

Security

Another essential component of society is that of a secure and safe refuge. Darwinism in many species promotes a "safety in numbers" genetic filter, giving many populations favor should they act as a unit. Social grouping makes mate selection and infant care easier, resources can be shared, acquired experience can be passed on, and outside threats can be more easily deterred.

Possibly the most primal human aspect carried into modern age is that of maintaining civil security, an alabaster wall that keeps our loved ones safe from the rival tribes and beasts that would otherwise usurp our lands and resources. Protectionism is so deeply ingrained in the purpose of civilization that it is often a dominant trait by which a nation defines itself.

Most notably, a secure and protected society has allowed for massive leaps in the application of acquired experience. Thousands of generations of people have built the mantle for modern man, their lives and experiences giving us everything from antibiotics to smartphones to space travel. Without safe space to conduct cultural and technological practice, there could be no significant experiential growth in a population. Even the prospect of ancient humans passing along the gift of fire to their children would have eventually been lost.

Providing security isn't always for the purpose of deterring external foes. The use of common law is also a means of security. While the question of, security for whom? could be posed (depending on the society in question), the use of law has guided the hand of civilized progress. The law should prevent social peers from harming one another, causing a regression of the societal state, or undermining notable acquired experience. For example, one shouldn't be allowed to murder, destroy infrastructure, or sell known poisonous foods.

Considering the idea of security as a cornerstone of society it comes as no surprise that the expansion of military and law enforcement has always been a major factor in the growth of civilizations. A buildup of security measures and personnel is a display of power that often encourages population booms, some degree of economic growth, and patriotism.

A phenomenal case study on the effects of security through a larger social context comes from one of nature's own experiments, based on the dividing line of the Congo river in East Africa.

For thirty-four million years the Congo river has served as a geological barrier, separating the lush and resource-rich lands to its south from the dry and semi-barren lands to its north. This divide caused a split in an ancient species, a common ancestor to both the modern chimpanzee and their cousin the bonobo. To the south bonobos live in relative peace. They are primarily vegetarian, living in female-dominated troupes who have not shown evidence of rivalry with neighboring tribes. The rich amount of resources in their environment has allowed for a lifestyle quite contrary to their northern family members. Bonobos do not aggressively observe territory lines between groups, allowing for cross-boundary resource gathering and mating.

Chimpanzees are quite the opposite of their peace-loving counterparts to the south. Chimps live in strictly male-dominated societies and are well known for their vicious conduct toward rival clans. This includes organized tribal warfare (unique only to certain apes—including humans), cannibalism, and extremely fixed territory lines. North Congo chimp societies have been shaped by the lack of resources available to them, becoming obsessed with the land they control, monopolizing the mates they have access to, and removing competitors from their territories.

Noting that these apes are remarkably similar to humans in terms of genetics can relay a certain point about societal security.

Consider that nations with the widest reach of imperial overtaking were mostly small countries: Britain, Spain, France, Belgium, etc. These nations likely were faced with population growth that exceeded the provisional abilities of their land mass. Many of the world's colonized nations were much larger than their respective ward-states, such as India, China, Central Africa, Australia, and the Americas. Widely generalizing, many of these larger geographical areas did not have the same emphasis on the development of warfare as Europe did, nor the understanding of how creating subservience through the homogenization of culture could be used as a means of control. No doubt this cruelty is the human equivalent of our northern chimpanzees. If chimps ever were to make it across the Congo they would brutalize their bonobo cousins.

While security is important to all societies, it becomes even more prevalent when there is a lack of necessities. The idea of starving, dehydration, and rival troupes has made the chimpanzee complicit with a hellish and violent way of life. In human beings this is most certainly supplemented by greed and avarice, but the parallel is still astounding. Consider the various indigenous tribes of North America, many of whom had a powerful emphasis on their female leaders. On such a resource-rich continent, warfare as seen in Europe was foreign. When European settlers came from across the ocean, they understood a side of man that the Native American had sadly never seen, a capability that was primal and malicious.

In oppressive societies like those of the patriarchal chimpanzee, acquired experience isn't necessarily positive. Experience that is passed on generationally becomes an acceptance of the system in place, which can be hierarchical and stagnant. If national pride and the choice of a civilization's enemies define so much about national identities, it can be easy to inflate these ideas of rivalry, even invent them, for the purpose of consolidating power. This can be a direct means to alter the acquired experience of a population into benign acceptance of existing power structures.

As with liquidity, an idea meant to disperse power can work to its own detriment. While security in a society can allow for safe space to define ideas, laws, democracy, and general development, it can also be used as a means to seize control over complicit masses under potentially false pretenses. The use of moral debt can be used to provoke action, framing fear or empathy as a means for social discord. The idea that one must act to save another is rhetoric that can be manipulated in order to provide a safe haven for illicit state affairs, wars, economic bailouts, and more.

Moral debt is also accompanied by ego-related affirmation bias, a need to prove the altruism of a society's ethics. By imposing morals or acting upon them, one affirms their own ego and concept of self. This activity is gratifying on both the personal and national level.

Quoting from Umberto Eco's *Inventing the Enemy* (2012):

Having an enemy is important not only to define our identity but also to provide us with an obstacle against which to measure our system of values and, in seeking to overcome it, to demonstrate our own worth. So when there is no enemy, we have to invent one.

Security and state expansion go hand in hand with a cyclical quality. Historically speaking, the vast amount of a civilization's tax base is directed toward military and protectionist rhetoric. As funding grows for military use, the state grows as well, becoming an ever-expanding synergetic entity. The job prospects of military work become more appealing to the populace and the perks of such employment also heavily diversify. More civilians join the security job field, overall security spending increases, and the state grows yet again. This mutually beneficial relationship doesn't often allow for a crucial reality to be analyzed, that being whether any part of the security state or spending is vestigial. No one wishes to lose their job, and no subdivision of government wishes to become defunct, making reasonable analysis near impossible for the exact and true needs of national security.

Just as with liquidity, the larger a society is, the more varied security needs become. Multinational economic entities have become just as influential as actual nations. By way of lobbying and political sponsorships, it is notable that these groups can influence national security and the surrounding rhetoric effectively. The internet has become the primary source of economic and social growth, opening up an entirely new front that requires security from hacking and illegal activity. As the needs for security diversify, the state responds with growth.

The growth of state has perpetuated so far in the modern world that organizations such as the United Nations have been instated to provide universal security amongst multiple states. Alliance treaties such as NATO outlive their counterparts like the Warsaw Pact, and mercenary-esque private security firms are heavily employed in global affairs.

The drive for security in a nation is both necessary and dangerous. Nationalist zealotry often stems from a feeling that security of state has failed, allowing outsiders to pollute an economy, nation, or ideology. From ancient caves to futuristic city skylines, human beings are extremely creative in our methods to secure society, holding tight to a primordial and basic instinct: to survive.

Public Forum

Having a secured and protected state allows for the foundation of the public forum to exist. When the main concerns of civilized individuals are not those of immediate survival, attention can be dedicated to the discussion of how to improve society or build social bonds. From a proper legislature, to a city square, to a local pub, public forums propagate the great zeitgeists of human history. Public forums allow for expansion and detailing of both security and liquidity, while also providing discussion pertaining to the values of a nation. It is in these environments that every major alteration of religion, politics, economics, and social conduct occurs. Think of every venue, from a concert arena, to Wall Street.

A most demonstrative example of the use of the public forum was illustrated by the rise of Greek democracy in the fifth century BC. While proto-democratic systems had existed elsewhere, like India, Mesopotamia, and Sparta, the Grecian democracy was far more pervasive in terms of ethics rather than tribal functionality. Philosophically, democracy rang as a beacon that political participation and individualism were intrinsic human rights. While this was still limited to (non-slave) males of a certain age it still showed far more progressivism than most civilizations to date.

Prior to the installation of democracy in Greece, public forums allowed for Grecian citizens to rally behind the mutual feeling that an aristocratic elite had been hoarding wealth while leaving the masses poorly taken care of. With such a lack of faith in their leadership, a revolution became inevitable. A disenchanted oligarch, Cleisthenes, sought to dismantle the aristocratic factions of Greece by organizing the people for popular vote by their *deme* or localized district.

True democratic interaction is one of the purest forms of public forum, permitting mass involvement in the craft of legislation. Suddenly every decision to alter law, economy, or ethics is a group decision that is discussed amongst all complicit members of a society. The evolution of public forums may have initially been meant for furthering economy and socialization, but the evolution of group politics was destined to be a trend that would dominate the overall path of civilized progress.

Interestingly enough there was also very rational dissent toward democratic process, namely from the mouths of Socrates, Aristotle, and Plato.

An excerpt from Plato's *Republic* (381 BC):

Democracy, which is a charming form of government,
full of variety and disorder, and dispensing a sort of
equality to equals and unequaled alike.

The great philosophers held great issue with democracy. This rested in a general feeling that the masses were not well informed enough of state affairs to effectively guide such dealings. To Plato, democracy posed the threat of being ruled by a majority with severe lack of political understanding. This isn't to say that a well-functioning democracy couldn't be possible, for instance a democracy that provides heavy emphasis on economic and political education.

Another quote is loosely attributed to Aristotle:

Republics decline into democracies and democracies
degenerate into despotisms.

While extremely absolutist in his convictions, Aristotle detailed well in this quote the potential for morphology in politics. This can also be heard in the rumored rhetoric of Vladimir Lenin on capitalism:

Fascism is capitalism in decay.

Each of these insights is not only derived from political dialogue in the public forum, but it also touches on the very center of the public forum's purpose. A dissident opinion regarding the public forum or democratic participation is in itself a great service to a society. From such words societies may take heed of warnings, observations, critiques, and successes. These criticisms serve to fine-tune political and social processes, an immensely valuable service for civil growth.

Just as a human being changes throughout their lifetime, so do political structures and hierarchies. There is no governance that remains static in its convictions or procedures, and as such the public forum remains a significant system for checking and balancing operating powers.

The expansion of the private sector in a nation greatly benefits the diversity of public forums, as marginalized groups can then build their own micro-communities and economies, greatly increasing the collective power of their political voices.

The human condition demands a sort of power consolidation, often through the means of kin selection or reciprocal altruism. As the great philosophers illustrated there is a well-warranted concern over pure and sudden democratic change.

The opposition to the democratic process and public forum can often be state sponsored as well, for the purposes of directly removing political pluralism.

One way this is done is through direct action against said pluralism. Because the creation of a public forum is as easy as men and women coming together for a specific social purpose, the destruction of a public forum's infrastructure can derail its function. Controversial examples could include the Black Wall Street of Tulsa circa 1921, the Philadelphia bombings of 1985, or the destruction of religious institutions in the Soviet Union.

Each is an example of systemic assistance in eliminating a public forum as a means to limit or curb societal dialogue, effectively preventing upward mobility for a group of people or an ideology. With the above listed incidents, direct action is very blunt and obvious: an organized group associated with entrenched power aims to destroy a purposeful forum. Each example cites conduct of government organizations aiding in the effort to remove fledgling economic or ideological microcosms.

More covertly, the act of espionage can be easily used to disrupt and misrepresent public forums. Should a government or politically active group be at odds with the message and conduct of a public forum, it can be easily derailed from within.

By posing as a participant in a public forum, an undercover individual may act violently or disturbingly, thereby promoting a public image of the forum movement as dangerous or immature. It is no exaggeration that something this simple can (and has) sabotaged entire social and economic movements. A perfect illustration is provided by the 2013 pro-EU protests in Kiev, Ukraine.

At the time of these protests, the Ukrainian government had opposed integration with the European Union trade bloc; an unpopular political move amongst the Ukrainian people. The response to this was predictable, namely that massive protests would ensue with epicenters at public forums such as Mariinsky Park. The citizenry itself appeared peaceful during the formative days of protest. However, it did not take long for the uproar to provide sanction for more zealous groups to take hold.

Far right conservative parties such as the Svoboda Nationalists and the Azov Battalion took this opportunity to enact a violent agenda and spark clashes with the Ukrainian government, using the pretense of mass protest as cover and license. With the aid of other factions and private security firms, the government was subject to a coup led by Svoboda, all of this stemming from the unassuming actions of average, nonviolent citizens who were exercising their right to protest.

Another means of causing public forum dispersion is through media portrayal. The use of media outlets to misrepresent, fabricate, and otherwise dilute the meaning or purpose of forum gatherings is as easy to do as it is effective.

Tying into the state's need for war, the Bureau of Investigative Journalism exposed in 2016 the use of US taxpayer money to create falsified terrorist videos by the Pentagon. This amounted to the tune of $540 million dollars, and most likely is not the first instance of these tactics. While some footage was purely falsified, the misuse of actual videos or images from war zones can often be mislabeled to contribute to a specific state-sponsored agenda. Images of protests from Venezuela can be labeled and marketed as if they were in Ferguson, Missouri, to entice public support for a more robust use of authoritative power. Scenes from a sarin gas attack during the Iraq-Iran War can be redistributed and sold as pictures from modern-day Syria, creating moral debt amongst Americans for the purpose of promoting military intervention.

A final method to disintegrate a public forum can be illustrated through government opposition to the Black Panther movement, a revolutionary socialist group of African-Americans. The Panthers were established in 1966 and promoted militant self-defense as protection from racist law enforcement, and for the purposes of neighborhood security. The Panthers also endorsed self-sufficient black economies in America.

Viewing this from the perspectives of liquidity and security, African-Americans were marginalized in the US to the point that they needed to reevaluate their status as constituent members of the society. This helped to draw the conclusion that state-sponsored services like law enforcement and economic participation were not as accessible or functional to the black community, and as such, new societal lines had to be drawn.

The display of power shown by the Black Panther movement drew a lot of attention from government organizations, the Central Intelligence Agency in particular. In response, these government organizations began the import of drugs to black neighborhoods and incited violence within the black community.

Closely linked to American ties with the Nicaraguan Contras in the 1980s, many whistleblowers have attested to government involvement in trafficking drugs to the inner cities of America. These included senator John Kerry, senator Gary Hart, Oliver North, DEA agent Celerino Castillo, and various drug industry personnel of both US and Nicaraguan descent. Even Juan Pablo Henao, the son of Pablo Escobar, alluded in 2016 that his father had business ties to the CIA, exchanging drugs for weapons to be used in his fight against the Colombian government.

This is not to imply that government is the only entity that carries interest in removing certain public forums. In fact, many institutions of government facilitate the existence of public forums and often provide sanctuary for such forums to exist. It is noteworthy to consider that by citizens giving a monopolization of power to their governments, they also give their government the ability to limit political pluralism in public forums.

Development

The final addition to our four societal foundations is the need for development. Liquidity, security, and the public forum all assist in manifesting a larger overall goal, that being the goal of renovating civilization into something that promotes a better quality of life to more people. Development can be both helped and hindered by its respective society, depending on the state of the other three foundations. Besides the obvious developmental boons in human history such as the creation of tools, fire, and role delegation in society, development is intimately linked to education.

The idea of a baseline education for the youth in a civilized group helps in the effort to have all persons working toward the goal of social evolution. While all societies still have conditions and limits to what individuals can do (based on hierarchy, access to liquidity or resources, etc.), a baseline education also allows for a shotgun approach to social roles. This ideally allows people to gravitate toward what they are best at, giving individuals (and thus the whole of society) a better group of scientists, carpenters, hunters, or engineers.

Developmental revolutions can be grouped into three major types.

The first occurred around 10,000 BC in the transition from hunter-gatherer tribalism to static and sustained agriculture amongst societies. The first agricultural revolution permitted a stable paradigm needed for liquidity, security, and the public forum to flourish. With the domestication of livestock and use of acquired experience to convey how to sustain crops, human civilizations could become much larger than previously seen in nomadic groups. Other agricultural revolutions continued to arise as the diaspora of civilizations grew;

crops exchanged around the world, and the art of cultivation was whittled down more perfectly with each generation. Arab, British, Scottish, Chinese, and other modern agricultural revolutions saw a rise in food output and a decrease in poverty per capita in many parts of the world.

The rise of static agriculture also laid the framework for deeper cultural growth, as many religious and ethnic subdivisions used references to the environment to display their identity. One of the most poignant showcases of this is the concept of a "sun god," the "son of god," or the "rebirth of the sun," all of which cite the winter solstice. During this time the earth ends its hemispheric tilt away from the sun and days become longer once again, prompting a feeling amongst ancient peoples of hope and looming prosperity for the upcoming sowing and harvest of their agriculture. Occurring between December 21 and December 31 in the Northern Hemisphere, it is no surprise that the allegorical birth of many sun gods coincide with this astrological event.

The underlying metaphor for the birth of these sun gods is that the sun dies during the winter, only to be reborn again after the solstice. Its rebirth signifies the boons of the coming year, and an assured end to the lean winter months.

Civilized identities no doubt became more and more detailed as a result of sustained agriculture. These events also marked a notable increase in average lifespan as well as successful birth rates, enabling population booms. The accessibility of needed nutrition and growth of medical sciences are inextricably linked to agricultural stability.

These advances were not without their critics. One in particular, Thomas Malthus, has been a recurring voice in the global dialogue of societal development and sustained growth. Malthus was an English scholar in the nineteenth century, and a bright mind specializing in macroeconomics. One of his considerations regarding sustained agriculture and population growth was written in *An Essay on the Principle of Population* (1798), wherein he characterized an impending catastrophe based on the discrepancy between birth rate and available necessities. According to Malthus, the rise in food production would inevitably lead to unprecedented population gains in the middle and lower class. This would prove to be an unbalanced equation, as the population explosion would eventually outweigh a nation's ability to produce necessities, thereby contradicting the ideal that life quality would continue to improve for everyone in an organized society. His rhetoric became a much-debated talking point for powerful figures such as Charles Darwin and Alfred Russel Wallace.

As one may imagine, Malthus's proposed restraints on reproduction (including legal limitations, sterilization, and general culling of the masses) had elitist and morally debatable undertones. Even in the modern world, his thoughts pervade much of the rhetoric on overpopulation, health infrastructure in the third world, and NGO dealings.

What Thomas Malthus did not take into account was a second developmental paradigm shift—that of the industrial revolutions. Between the late 1700s and 1850 the process of manufacturing goods became so streamlined that machines took on the role of manual labor. Tasks that once had to be done by hand could now be transferred to means of mass production, inventions powered by steam and water. Everything from lumber, to food, iron, and textiles were now easier to produce en masse and arrived on the market faster, giving rise to consumer revolutions in their wake.

The institution of marriage also morphed as many young people began to marry later in life, allowing them to accumulate more wealth before starting a family.

These permutations of economy and growth created an output of goods that had never been seen before, prompting more and more individuals to specialize in services and recreational trade. Markets like these expanded greatly due to the new shift in labor, and the impending Malthusian catastrophe became a more distant prospect.

Out of this also came a new and intense duality. While the offset of manual labor and increased production of goods gave an upward climb in life quality, the industrial revolution also provided the opportunity for a newfound global elite to manifest as a worldwide power.

The decentralization of national powers gave way to a centralization of economic powers that had multinational capabilities. Due to the massive capital needed for industrial manufacture, it was easy for affluent families and groups to monopolize many industries, buying out their potential competitors or lobbying governments to create detrimental legislation aimed at smaller entrepreneurs.

In the famous case of Thomas Alva Edison and pseudo-rival Nikola Tesla, Edison went to extreme means to preserve his monopoly on many applied sciences. Electricity at the time was limited to direct current (or DC), the primary means for which were supplied in the US by Edison's company Edison Electric (eventually becoming General Electric after an acquisition by J. P. Morgan). DC was a difficult mode of transfer for electricity, requiring many power plants throughout their desired range and having a limited spectrum of voltages to choose from. This of course created limitations in the market for what could be powered by electricity, as well as what geographically could be zoned as residential or commercial.

However, the market for electricity itself had variations that were competing for dominance.

Nikola Tesla was one of several inventors who had created an alternating current, or AC, that had the means to bypass many DC limitations. With the use of a step up or step down transformer, electric current could be modified without a power plant every few miles, allowing voltage to be regulated for a wider variety of uses with far less capacity for the dangerous potentials DC possessed.

This development was not ideal for Edison, who collaborated with many of his counterparts to create a smear campaign directed at AC. This included publicity campaigns, faked deaths, and the public electrocution of animals, all citing exaggerated dangers of AC. Tesla's business suffered, and eventually the patents to alternating current would be acquired by General Electric and a few other large electric companies, most of which are still in operation.

The final shift in development references a second coming of industrial revolutions, a version far more streamlined with an increased and exponential effectiveness. A technological revolution describes building upon an existing industrial revolution. For instance, consider the printing press.

Prior to industrialized newspaper printing, each letter of a document had to be hand pressed upon paper, no doubt an arduous task. With the invention of the printing press, lettering became industrialized, an application of industrial revolution. Output of documented lettering increased, and manual labor for printing was no longer in demand.

Building upon this development came the modernized means of communication and documentation—the internet. A massive technological advancement, online access to lettering allowed individuals to read a plethora of material without the need for physical printed goods such as newspapers, bound books, or magazines. This streamlining of informational process forced the industry of physical printing to change or become functionless.

The internet also paved the way for a new democratic process in which anyone can post their opinion, business ad, or personal thoughts on a well-defined and accessible media; unlike the limited means that were possible under the printing press. Suddenly democratic participation wasn't limited to subjective pundits; rather, anyone could join in on the conversation and contribute to the largest public forum in history.

The three developmental shifts all work in tandem to further a societal ideal and raise the effectiveness of liquidity, security, and the public forum.

Notes

Each foundation of societal growth is a necessary protocol to progress in a society. They are not without their flaws and can be used for both consolidation and deconsolidation of power structures. Without a lens of objectivity, rhetoric can be easily skewed to pollute the true use of these important building blocks. As social creatures, human beings must not only recognize the impact and need for liquidity, security, the public forum, and development, but we must also strive for a more unified and recognizable interchange between these civil gears. Each will contribute in determining the efficacy of a nation, and ultimately the global community as a whole.

Liquidity in particular has been a driving force in the removal of vestigial power, giving individuals the potential for immense social growth. The author of the Harry Potter book series, J. K. Rowling, provides an extreme example.

Rising from a lower-middle class background to a net worth between 600 million and $1 billion, Rowling has become a larger economic force than the Queen of England, whose net worth is estimated at around $500 million. By promoting variations on liquidity, the world has propelled itself beyond rigid hierarchy and disposed of preconceived notions that one individual is intrinsically more valuable than another.

Most notably with each of these foundations is the capacity for dissident opinion and change being used to improve their function. The medium of exchange in liquidity, the integrity of power monopoly in security, the settings of the public forum, and the reincarnations of development all suggest that the most powerful societal attribute of humanity is the ability to change.

Much as the concept of evolution drives living organisms, so must we allow evolutions to drive the state of our communities. Stagnant structures of any of our four foundations will ultimately lead to dysfunction and regressive despotism. Consequently, it must be of primary concern that even above tradition, variation and change are revered amongst those in civilized society; giving leeway to more successful designs while learning from the boons and busts of history.

Great nations like ancient Greece and Rome had long-standing infrastructure, including aqueducts and wide-spanning advanced economic control. However, after the fall of Rome, the Dark Ages marginalized many former Roman territories into splintered feudal cells, losing much of the sanitary, philosophical, and technological advances that such nations had made.

The result was a regression of state and life quality—opening the doors to rampant disease, famine, poor education, and widespread population loss. Through their power grabs the feudal leaders of the Dark Ages inadvertently stomped upon the benefits laid before them by prior civilizations, ensuring a short and harsh span of life for their societies.

By virtue of having these four foundations a civilization is free to shape its rhetoric and function around them. Systems of liquidity, security, public forum, and development help to determine their surrounding style of government: authoritarianism, libertarianism, capitalism, communism, democratic republicanism, and state capitalism.

Government

*While all other sciences have advanced, that of
government is at a standstill—little better understood,
little better practiced now than three or four thousand
years ago.*
—John Adams

*Our government . . . teaches the whole people by its
example. If the government becomes the lawbreaker, it
breeds contempt for law; it invites every man to become
a law unto himself; it invites anarchy.*
—Louis D. Brandeis

*It is not the function of the government to stop the
citizen from falling into error; it is the function of the
citizen to keep the government from falling into error.*
—Justice Robert Jackson, judge at the Nuremberg trials

*And on the subject of burning books: I want to
congratulate librarians, not famous for their physical
strength or their powerful political connections or their
great wealth, who, all over this country, have staunchly
resisted anti-democratic bullies who have tried to
remove certain books from their shelves, and have
refused to reveal to thought police the names of persons
who have checked out those titles.*

*So the America I loved still exists, if not in the White
House or the Supreme Court or the Senate or the House
of Representatives or the media. The America I love
still exists at the front desks of our public libraries.*
—Kurt Vonnegut

After the construction of the four foundations required for large-scale society, constituents and leaders are now faced with a variety of choices. What sort of society can they create? What binds its moral fibers? What precedence will it assign to its various social and economic groups? What is the legacy this nation wishes to lead?

The answer is rarely unanimous. Often we see hybridized governments instead of purified structures, a mix of design and procedure that draws from many sources—both visible and hidden. This is where practicality fuses with philosophy, manifesting a wide variety of outcomes depending on an even wider array of variables.

Other such questions that may affect government effectiveness could address the surrounding geography, the ethnic or racial margins within the society, the GDP or sources of income, its historical or nationalist background, and many more components.

The philosophical system that a civilization believes in heavily determines its economic and procedural function. A sense of equality for all citizens will create a different society than something based on hierarchy. Religious institutions sanctioned by government may offer preferred political status to their followers. Moral debt can be a massive means of persuasion if emphasized by the rhetoric of its surrounding culture. Philosophy aids in the ability to create identity, and a nation devoid of identity is destined to fail.

The many variations of humanity assure that world governments rarely assume the same form. Much as with individual people it is difficult, if not impossible, to designate wide or generalized groupings for a nation's modus operandi.

The following aims to provide a clear and transparent basis for analysis of government systems. Each grouping is meant to provide a polarized spectrum between a system and its opposite, though postulating that such binaries truly exist is far too simple. A system of governance can either illustrate a reflection of the society that harbors it or assume a form of monopolized power, forcibly exerting itself over constituents.

Authoritarianism, Libertarianism

A central choice in political philosophy is that of self-determination vs. established-determination. A society that deems self-determination to be paramount likely prefers a kind of democratic process, representative officials, open social rights, and a widely varied economy. Individualism is deemed extremely important, as is expression of self. Validation comes from succeeding in personal endeavors and economic or artistic finesse.

Established-determination implies a state decision upon the values, economy, social standards, and acceptable periphery of a nation's people. These societies tend to prefer dynastic or dictatorial leadership, a strong emphasis on national well-being over the wants of the individual, limited social rights, and a strictly managed range of economy.

A main rhetorical point for established-determinative politics is that self-determinative culture leads to ego-centrism. Social dysfunction is attributed to selfish personal desires, placing blame for economic or political issues upon individuals who seek non-unified goals. In the wake of such practices, the masses may endorse a more centralized leadership, with whom they share a vision for a more practical and streamlined nation.

With such a viewpoint it is realistic to see a central and powerful government as being an avenue to eliminate political branches that are seeded with corruption, and unify the goals of the people, rather than encouraging them to disperse toward individualistic aims. In a sense established-determination is meant to homogenize government with the intention of cleansing unneeded bureaucratic symptoms.

Contrarily, self-determination is often the backlash from an oppressive or established system. The act of creating activistic art or the use of public forums by marginalized groups often accompanies established-determinative structures, as those who do not share single-minded national goals lash out.

Dually, a system that solely embraces self-determination can often overlook the realities regarding government as business in the world marketplace. If all individuals seek to become artists, celebrities, or things purely self-fulfilling, no one is left for the manual labor needed to preserve infrastructure, much less the demand for GDP.

The progressivism of self-determination is better suited to satiate the needs of more people, especially as the global community becomes increasingly secular. The underlying issue is that means of national preservation for the economy and culture can become diluted in an overly individualistic society—demonstrating the push and pull of authoritarianism and libertarianism.

The establishment of unified government rests upon a general agreement amongst the masses for monopolized use of force. In other words: the constituents of a nation must all be complicit with their country having a fixed and official structure of authority, and one that is capable of exercising the use of force. A stable society must inherently remove a measure of political pluralism to function. Unsanctioned factions are a liability to the well-being of an established government. It is upon this concept that authoritarianism flourishes, being a creature of single-toned and strict decorum.

Building upon the removal of political pluralism, an authoritarian regime operates off of a powerful executive branch that often removes or usurps the power of other political branches. Writing and passing law (the job of the legislature) or interpreting/applying law (the job of the judiciary) can be consolidated to a single operative.

Accompanying this consolidation is the minimizing of social dialogue, including limitation of public forum as well as other societal foundations. Depending on the authoritarian leader this can lead to foundational degradation. In earlier history (even up until the twentieth century) dynastic, dictatorial leadership was not unusual. Much of this was due to the great philosophers' consideration that democratic process or self-determination was a liability, unless education in macro affairs could be accurately given. The masses of many given nations were kept in the dark as to how they could effectively run their own countries, allowing an elite group or family to reign for extended periods of time. Kin selection and reciprocal altruism kept these ruling circles small. Emphasis on nationalism gave more energy to this cycle, advocating a loyalty to the royal family and a perceived (and promoted) familial relationship between the constituents of a nation.

What led to the end of many authoritarian dynasties were the various industrial revolutions and their subsequent globalization of economics. The dilution of dynastic rule occurred throughout Europe by no coincidence during one of the largest industrial revolutions in history. As workers became more skilled in the operation of complex machinery, powerful economic moguls stripped the monopoly of power and influence from global royalty, creating a new world imparted with fresh philosophical ideals. It is with these ideals that new political ideologies began to take hold and varying ideas of class mobilization became manifest through a series of revolutions. Two of the most dynamic shifts were those of the Weimar Republic in Germany and the Soviet Union in Russia.

Russia is a nation with an incredibly diverse national history. With Far Eastern influences from their occupation by the Mongolians, an enormous territory of Slavic/eastern European nations, the Jewish diaspora, and various migrants from the Baltic, Russia has always been a tremendously secular nation.

The presiding Russian royalty prior to the October Revolution (the tsars) operated a heavily tiered society wherein familial, state, military, and religious officials all had more rights and resources than the average Russian citizen. Upward class mobility was confined to only select officials, leaving great spans of the Russian nation subject to poverty and dismal social monotony.

As political philosophies of equality emerged, they were destined to gain immediate and powerful traction. The libertarian backlash against the tsars promised an equal share of Russia's gains and spoils, advocating true reward to everyone for the toils of the individual. Led by revolutionists like Vladimir Lenin, Leon Trotsky, and Rosa Luxemburg, a pristine ideal emerged to place uniform equality at the helm of a new Russia.

However, in this desire to break the chains of authoritarian dynasty an alternate established-determination was created.

When the revolution was completed there was intense dismissal of organized religion, citing that a belief in God undermined true allegiance to the state. The Orthodox Church had enjoyed a very pampered treatment under tsarist rule, and its lavish conduct had fostered an extreme animosity from the new revolutionary government.

Dissident opinion toward the state and its widening bureaucracy was considered treasonous by the rising Communist Party, leaving little space for meaningful evolution in politics. As such, means for security and development were reforged as tools to suppress public forums rather than enhance them.

While the Red Revolution may have had libertarian tones on the outset, it fostered a different kind of authoritarian rule in many ways. This regime could be called leftist authoritarian, as conceptually the strict hand of government was meant rhetorically to apply a more equal classism to the masses.

The concept of state-mandated equality functions on practices that make the government a facet in almost every social exchange. For example, a man that mines iron may have to turn it over to the state so they could allocate it properly and fairly to the surrounding region. This can create an impersonal and ineffective middle man government position. As overinflated government takes many cultivated necessities to distribute as necessary, it becomes easy to overlook true regional requirements for food, water, medicine, and much else.

However it is also integral to note that the nations who have utilized this described system did so by quickly changing from largely agrarian societies into industrial powerhouses almost overnight. Dialecticians such as Karl Marx argued that the decentralized nature of the free market could eventually provide a good platform for his ideals (in other words, Marx asserted that capitalism could very well be a prerequisite for communism).

That notwithstanding- the people's revolution dreamed of by figures like Lenin, Luxemburg, and Trotsky were undermined over time by the very bureaucracy they helped to create, becoming a true authoritarian despotism under Joseph Stalin.

The Weimar Republic (predecessor to Nazi Germany) had a similar tale, but with a very different twist. Kaiser Wilhelm II, a man who had made very controversial decisions during World War I, was the last German emperor prior to the November Revolution in Germany. His sense of decorum and wartime decision-making was in constant question. It came as no surprise that he had lost the faith of the German Army in 1918. After his abdication and exile to the Netherlands, Germany elected to expand their liberties via a parliamentary system of representation. This meant that the public forum and development would have a much wider range of input than during the time of emperors and kings. The people of Germany were all meant to contribute to the self-determination of their state. The adopted system of economics became a type of free market, relatively unrestricted compared to the Soviets. While the promise of better life quality was given to the Germans, it did not imply equality. Instead it simply advertised that there would be potential for upward mobility, based on economic and societal success. It was decided that hierarchy could be tolerated, so long as that hierarchy permitted class mobility.

Building liquidity allowed for non-governmental entities to become influential in the Weimar Republic, diversifying power away from government consolidation. While the Soviets had deficits in the public forum and development, it would be in the foundations of liquidity and security that the Weimar Republic would crumble.

Despite the German monarchy being dismantled, Germany had an international debt to pay for its loss in the First World War. Damages throughout Europe were severe, and as repercussion the German government was made to sign the Treaty of Versailles. This legislation put the new republic under severe duress, in that it usurped German autonomy and demanded reparations be paid to the nations of Europe to rebuild the war-torn continent. National profits and resources that could've helped the German people were put to use elsewhere, and major national industries were bought out by foreign powers, some as far away as Wall Street in the United States. While there was more class diversity than there was under the monarchy, Germany still had a massive yoke hanging around its neck.

In response to this crisis, the Weimar government was grasping at straws for solutions. They settled upon an inflation of currency and de-standardizing from gold, creating more money to help stimulate the economy and domestic workforce. By spreading German liquidity too thin the Weimar was soon stuck with a currency that was incredibly weak, paling in comparison to foreign monies and barely able to provide citizens with enough for even basic exchange. The German mark then created a snowball effect upon itself as other European nations wanted WWI reparations to be paid in their own currencies, which became far greater in worth than what Germany had to offer.

The exchange rate discrepancy for reparations, coupled with desperate attempts at economic recovery through currency inflation, made a destitute and stagnant German economy. What the Weimar was left with would be a useless paper currency, intrinsically unable to purchase even a loaf of bread. Poverty and extreme class divide soon followed, leaving the German people in a furor that demanded a scapegoat.

It didn't take long for a nationalist thematic to take hold, blaming the poor state of the German public on foreign entities and lax social policy. The liberalism of the republic was to blame in the eyes of many Germans, namely state officials who had signed the Treaty of Versailles, designated "the November Criminals." This nefarious portrayal included civilians of non-German descent who were supposedly taking advantage of an overly-liberalized government, the operators of the Reichsbank who inflated the German mark, and the ever-expanding Soviet Union next door.

It is no coincidence that many people of Jewish lineage were also blamed, as several Reichsbank officials and treaty legislators were of Jewish heritage.

As the libertarian self-determinative Weimar Republic struggled, Adolf Hitler rose to power. He promised a government that would take care of native Germans and end the subjugation by foreign powers and alien residents. His words rang as beneficial to the masses of Germany, who were seeing conditions nearly as bad (or worse) as they had been under the monarchy. The idea of purging government branches and marginalized peoples seemed practical, as these entities were increasingly seen as valuing themselves over German livelihood, creating a fear-based political setting not unlike that of the Soviets.

Just as their communist neighbors did with the Orthodox Church, the Weimar began to demonize any who had allegiance to anything other than national German sovereignty. Eventually parliament burned to the ground, power was consolidated to a dictatorship, and the narrative of a need for increased national security ushered in the Third Reich.

It is a terrible and interesting thing to see the push and pull of libertarianism and authoritarianism. The four foundations can help each other grow, but can also sabotage each other quite easily.

For the Russians this meant that development and the public forum were stunted in the Soviet system, creating a hemorrhage in securing their ever-expanding borders and issuing basic necessities. Political and technological advancement (though quite impressive in the USSR) was also relatively stunted, as open discussion and non-state-sanctioned programs were illicit. Again, these considerations should be contrasted with the dialectics of Marx in his later years.

For the Germans this meant that liquidity and development were compromised, creating a terrible backlash of extreme security and shutting down of the public forum. The liquid means of economic exchange stopped working and any German development was usurped by foreign powers, leading Germans to clamp down on the public forum and raise security to a draconian level.

In each example we see clearly an authoritarian rule abolished, a replacement by left-leaning or right-leaning libertarian ideals, the decay of such ideals under foundational duress, and the eventual return to centralized authoritarianism.

Building upon such citations it can be examined what is true and false regarding libertarianism. A libertarian governance operates on premises that are nearly binary to the authoritarian. This includes a dispersal of state power (either through various political branches or outright abolishment), encouragement of social and ethnic diversity, and a focus upon individual rights as well as self-reliance. What often causes issues with libertarian movements goes beyond their political and economic implications, instead stemming from the literal geography of their origin.

The ideas surrounding libertarianism are often at odds with regionally entrenched cultural or societal values. Secular growth is nonnegotiable to implementing libertarian politics. Unequal treatment based on gender, sexuality, race, religion, or appearance all deter such augmentation.

Libertarianism has had many incarnations, yet the most elegant features can be contrasted between the Catalonian libertarian and the American libertarian. In an overview, these two libertarians can be classified as socialist and capitalist. The former defines their libertarian ideals as a means to expand socialist society, exemplified in wartime Catalonia, Spain, in the 1930s.

After the fall of the Spanish monarchy, Spain was governed by a leftist republic, which in turn was overthrown by a right-leaning military junta. It was during this military rule that Spain gave heavy support to the Axis powers in return for the assistance it had received from Germany during the Spanish Civil War. While supposedly neutral in World War II, the Spanish government led by General Francisco Franco had clear endorsement of both Benito Mussolini and Adolf Hitler. Predictably this overt Axis allegiance did not merit loyalty from all Spanish peoples, fostering a counterculture of libertarian backlash in the fiercely independent region of Catalonia.

Catalonians had a severe dislike for the emboldening of fascism, and were able to assemble their own army based on principles of self-governance and workers unions. These factions took control of their region and stripped power from the fascist military junta, imposing a political structure that was the literal opposite of the Spanish government.

While there was a central army meant to deter invaders, the regions of Catalonia were operated with total independence. Agrarian societies were loosely connected and governed by the people, or by a rotating democratic council. Thus, a new republic emerged out of Catalonia, advocating libertarianism and self-determination. The string that held these republics together was that of a socialist mentality, wherein a shared army was widely supported as was economic exchange. Responsibility to cultivate and disperse necessities was imperative, giving the separate republics common socialist ties. These programs were regionally implemented to help give equal access to resources, widen the middle class, and prevent austerity.

During the chaos unfolding between Catalonian libertarians and the fascist junta of Spain, American naval ships were deployed to oversee the events as moderators. Oddly enough they stopped supplies meant for the Catalonians, yet turned a blind eye to those meant for the junta. This was likely to prevent further reason for Spain to join the Axis. However it is notable that American entities openly supported Spanish fascism and helped to suppress Catalonian libertarianism.

As interesting as the Catalonian libertarian movement was it did not exist long enough to provide a good case study as to its effectiveness. The idea of a socialist libertarian government has caught much discussion in the world of political philosophy. Many even branded the movement as anarchist, in the meaning that there were no long-standing leaders or power structures. The constant movement of authoritative positions likely helped to cleanse negative effects of entrenched power, but without a long-standing model it's tough to say. This saga was a reasonable fallout from the military rule, and even more so predictable given that post-civil war Spain had been divided between Anglophiles and Germanophiles.

Germany had helped immensely in the Spanish Civil War, and advocates of a more authoritarian Spanish state were sympathetic to the Axis cause. Those who were more in favor of a republic-style rule were obviously at odds with the junta government and Axis, not to mention the immediate geography of Spain put it at the Allies' doorstep. Spanish sympathies during the war were divided as such, creating a climate that heavily implied domestic discord.

As the twentieth century progressed American libertarianism developed its own identity. As with its Catalonian cousin, American libertarianism stands heavily on the concepts of decentralized government, social/secular tolerance, and self-determinism. The difference between the two lies less in philosophy and more in execution. While the Catalonians allowed their small republics to collect and help to distribute wealth and necessities, the American libertarian focuses upon private enterprise. A key idea behind these politics is an extreme limitation of government, including the abolishment of many socialist constructs. The American libertarian is so keen on free-market economics that a purist may argue that government function is unnecessary in a diverse economy, and that federal oversight could be replaced by private enterprises with the voting consent of the people.

For example, roads could be maintained and constructed by private organizations rather than government affiliates. If a company were to do a subpar job they could be replaced by effective competitors. While there is little presence of government-provided social programs, American libertarianism promotes ingenuity in the free market for the purpose of rendering government ineffective.

Another key note of libertarian mentality in the USA is fiscal conservatism and the re-standardization of gold to the US dollar. Key libertarian politicians like Ron Paul tirelessly reference Austrian economists such as Ludwig von Mises, who was famous in his convictions against socialism, the promotion of restrictive banking regulations, and the need for currency standardization. Many of these ideologies can also be likened to historical figures like John Locke and Thomas Jefferson.

In essence, this American hybrid libertarian is supremely focused upon their perception of practicality above equal rights. While democratic action could still be used, the docket of public works would be limited to private enterprise far more than government. This decision results from the observation that government bureaucracy frequently goes hand in hand with wasteful spending and vestigial models of development. Implementation of term limits could also be considered libertarian styled means to hinder entrenched power, government abuse, or coercion. These considerations do not, however, consider the waste and abuse that can exist within privately held companies, or the disproportionate access to opportunities based on holdings of capital.

While the limitation of federal powers may yield much more freedom for development and liquidity, it is not without its own reasonable concern. Government oversight may limit free-market activity, but it can also ensure an equal playing field for more constituents via regulatory legislation. In a purely American libertarian nation the only standards for operation would be set by businesses and companies individually, leaving a lot of grey area for potentially exclusionary or dangerous practices. The only saving grace to this would be the promise of free-market economics allowing poor businesses to fail and be replaced by better models. Yet this hinges upon the morals and demands of buyers, of which there is no promise for potent action.

For instance, if alcohol weren't subject to government regulations it could have very dangerous side effects. Without a set standard of quality and production consumers run the risk of being poisoned or going blind. Government can act as a means of applying acquired experience across a broad spectrum, so as to ensure public safety en masse.

While American libertarianism relies upon a classical liberal standpoint economically, Catalonian libertarianism seems to have trended the opposite way. One incarnation promotes economic freedom to the extreme, while the other has pseudo-socialist demands to be met. Both believe highly in individual responsibility, social freedoms, a limitation of authoritative government, and a cycling of power structures. A caveat for such ideals would address how over-liberalized economics may not ensure that basic social/liquidity based needs of the masses are met. The free market could potentially correct these issues, but it would take time. Working out the kinks in such a loosely connected society would require highly integrated networks for private companies to meet civilian needs—or risk revolutionary social reform that could lead back to authoritarian governance. Were a libertarian society to come under scrutiny regarding its operation, the political backlash would most likely be in favor of government expansion and power consolidation.

It is for this reason that experiments into the world of a fully libertarian society are cut short, and political growth on this side of the spectrum is slow. The modern world of globalization gives new life to such prospects, as individual liberty and market diversity grow. The next century will provide meaningful insight into the possibility of consistent individual needs being met effectively by libertarian ideals. What has also yet to be seen is the amount of government regulation that would be necessary to provide foundational security in such a scenario.

Capitalism, Communism

Self-determinism and established-determinism are dueling mentalities that contribute to communist and capitalist societies. The implementation of either structure lies in a philosophical bedrock that must be shared by the majority of a nation's people. They can exist with either authoritarian or libertarian partnering.

These two mentalities have both existed in some form throughout history, but modernized society has inflated and hyper-extended both models. In turn this has provided valuable insight into their practical nature in terms of large-scale civilization. Dichotomies between communism and capitalism can be condensed by comparing their abilities to produce higher quality development, better security for the state, widening equality amongst their populace, and their environmental impact.

Fully adopting either model has historically required the minimizing or abolition of monarchic hierarchy, making the great experiment between the two take place after the twentieth-century European revolutions.

As mentioned before, the Weimar Republic and Soviet Union had contrasting views of what to do after their respective revolutions. The rationality behind the two mindsets was as follows.

For the future communists, the reality of inequality under the tsars fostered a demand for equal treatment among all Russians. Under minds like Karl Marx and his contemporaries, a desire arose to create a society that provided benefits to all hard-working Soviet members.

The thought behind communism in Russia, China, Vietnam, Cambodia, Cuba, and other nations is quite altruistic. Ideally, the concept was to unite the efforts of all peoples in a nation toward the betterment of their economy, technologies, and resource integration. By putting all the effort for development behind one workforce (rather than through the combative nature of the free market), communists surmise that the great minds of a nation will work better together than apart. Economically the same assumption is reinforced. Should all peoples of a country work to better their GDP and industry, surely it would be to the benefit of the nation as a whole.

Contrasted with capitalism, many participants in capitalist society work for industry that is not directly tied to their respective nation. As a result these industries have little thought as to the impact of their practices in a public sense, having the ability to undermine national autonomy and progress.

With fair treatment across the board for communist citizenry, it was also a supposed given that all members of the nation would want to perform as efficiently as possible. The adage of "All for one and one for all" comes to mind. For the communists of the world this meant that no individual would be subject to preferred treatment. The people would succeed when the nation succeeded, and fail when the nation failed. By making the stakes high and clear-cut, complicity amongst communist masses is easily understood.

An extremely important side note to this is the environmental impact of modern society, which increased exponentially in the twentieth century. The industrial and technological revolutions saw massive changes in the way things were manufactured and procured. For instance, even though colonial acquisition of resources had existed for a very long time, the invention of mechanically operated mechanisms for harvesting made exports from across the world grow in size. More land was needed to cultivate raw materials, more fuel needed for the machines, and more ships for trade. In the major nations of the world industry was booming. Factories went up, smokestacks roared into action, and the demand for energy technology soared.

From the communist perspective a sudden drain of resources and energy seemed wasteful when in the hands of capitalists. With the demand of free market competition it seemed inevitable that greed and adversarial business practices would needlessly waste the earth's resources. Why have hundreds of choices of shoes to choose from when a single reliable company could fulfill everyone's needs? The overstock of shoes from those hundreds of competing companies could amount to massive amounts of unused footwear, trash, pollution, and manpower. Some communist rhetoric dictates that the idea of homogenizing industry helps to unify the population, as well as minimize society's destructive impact on the world.

As admirable as many of these ideals are they have shown considerable faults. Insofar as equality, the amount of regulations and bureaucracy needed to facilitate some forms of communism have shown tendencies to create an aristocratic elite. State officials that oversee executing and legislating communist governance often end up with a higher social standing than the average citizen, betraying a key principle of the ideology. This is followed by the natural human condition of opportunism, wherein an individual sees opportunity and seizes it. Bureaucratic officials often aggrandize their own salaries, consolidate wealth and power, or even make deals with foreign nations that subvert communist morality.

In authoritarian communist nations like those under Stalin, Mao Zedong, or Pol Pot, there was an extreme persecution of marginalized populations that led to mass executions. Most of these operated on the same pretense as the oppression of the Russian Orthodox Church under the Soviets, a general concept that no faith should be higher than one's faith in the communist state. While further examining these instances it is important to note that there is significant historical revisionism in the reported numbers of casualties. The influence of post Cold War anti-communist propaganda must be taken into account.

The assumption that the use of resources would be lessened under communism was correct in several ways. But just as there may have been a positive aspect to this, it also harbored serious drawbacks. Toward the end of World War II, Germany and Russia were locked in heavy conflict. Before the turning point in Stalingrad, it seemed as though the Nazis had the upper hand. Though there were fewer Nazi troops than there were Russians, the Nazis were better armed and prepared for battle with proper rations and medicine. The Soviets, by contrast, were running out of guns, boots, medicines, ration packs, and other basic needs for combat. A command from Joseph Stalin to the infantry was to enter the battleground unarmed and to pick up weapons from the fallen bodies of their comrades.

The Allies' solution to this supply shortage on the eastern front was to supplement the Russians with arms from the USA, via Siberia. The aid had to be shipped across the entire North Asian continent to be used on the warfront. That being said the stalwart and tenacious nature of Russian troops won the war in Europe, eventually dismantling the German front and ending the expansion of the Reich eastward. This was not without severe loss, as Russia lost 15 percent of its entire population, an estimated twenty-six million people. This painful reality begs the question of what may have been different if the Soviet army were sufficiently prepared with wartime necessities.

The Cold War also saw a rise in nuclear proliferation, creating gigantic amounts of toxic waste as well as incidents like Chernobyl. Toward the end of the Soviet Empire, it seemed as though environmental impact was of far less concern. The communist and capitalist saber-rattling that occurred across the world made for immense nuclear arsenal buildups, a terrible strain on both environment and economy.

For capitalists, monarchic governance was replaced by what is deemed as a more practical hierarchy. This new modus operandi of the state basically applied a sink or swim ultimatum to its people, where success in society depended on how useful an individual is to said society. For capitalists the removal of vestigial entities is a primary goal for societal success. The government is limited in its control over markets, and private business is encouraged to provide a wide array of choices to the public for their services and products. If a business or individual is not savvy in maintaining their own usefulness or liquidity, they are lowered in the social tiers. Those who obtain liquid assets become the controlling forces in the society, while those who lack liquid assets are of less influence. For development this meant that older, dysfunctional, obsolete, or corrupted models would crumble in the wake of more effective competitors in the market. Ideally the pretense of competition is meant to bring out the best in new technologies. It is assumed that having non-unified market competition will ensure that there is always an incentive for upward mobility and industrial progress.

In this scenario it becomes the role of government to prevent the monopoly of industry by overly-prominent companies. If an agency were to remove its competitors from the market and become the sole source of its product or service, development would be limited to that company's own progress, thereby undermining the rhetoric of capitalism. Through regulations and legislation that encourage small business a government could feasibly promote active capitalism in perpetuity.

Yet it is through these same concepts that capitalism can be deconstructed. If a major company controlled its own market so heavily that it could manipulate government legislation, a monopoly could be easily achieved. Were this the case, government and industry would work hand in hand toward established-determinism, a construct not terribly different from communism.

The self-determination of capitalism yields a massive selection of occupations, innovations, and products. As a result of globalized outsourcing for public demand, capitalism has ushered in a widening global middle class. Large-scale capitalist companies have the ability to provide infrastructure to job markets in locations worldwide; yet due to profit-based priorities they may also take advantage of people in many nations whose governments do not protect them. Those endless varieties of shoes to choose from in capitalist society may be part of a troublesome conundrum.

While capitalist factories in South Asia have given work to their respective populaces, pay and workplace safety may not have adequate oversight. Government regulations may not protect the workers or the environment, and in many cases it is the cheaper labor and lack of regulations that encourage capitalist industry to move to developing countries. It becomes the job of the consumer to responsibly consider and research the implications of their purchases and demands. Many of these corporate malpractices have been confronted and ceased due to civilian intervention, yet with such a diverse marketplace it seems an increasingly daunting task to oversee the intentions of all capitalist companies.

If these points are addressed and personal/environmental protection is established overseas, international industry could conversely be a way to coerce corrupted governments into modernizing and accepting standards of more reliable conduct.

Wasteful consumption and production are also in the realm of capitalist shortcomings. As privatized companies produce and sell their products, two primary obstacles occur. One is the contingency that demand will supersede supply; therefore a company will always create a surplus of supply. This is done in case there is significant demand for a product, yet if this is not the case there is a tremendous amount of physical and pollutive waste. The idea of production prior to actual, measured demand leaves the environment in a precarious position. When competitive economics are introduced a second problem becomes visible. A surplus of antiquated products in a market become unusable and have little potential for sale. This renders entire market inventories as trash, much of which is not eligible for recycling or reuse.

While capitalism yields physical waste, it also has the ability to limit fiscal government waste. A perfect example can be found in the dissolution of the Penn Central Transportation railroad company.

The twentieth century was destined to see the decline of passenger railroads. As personal vehicles became more accessible and the US government implemented the interstate system, personal transit through the railroads was subject to severe lack of business. Penn Central was such a large company that when it went bankrupt in 1976, the United States opted to bail the business out. This effectively made Penn Central's successors (Amtrak and Conrail) into government assets.

Conrail was eventually bought out by independent capitalist investors, leaving Amtrak in the hands of Washington. Conrail's investors pushed the use of their trains for commercial transportation, a service in much higher demand than passenger trains. As a result Conrail began to turn an eventual profit reaching well into the present. Amtrak, by contrast, still resides in heavy debt, subsidized yearly by the US government via taxpayer dollars. The safety net of government spending allows Amtrak to be a yearly burden to the average taxpayer, and despite the loss of market demand this vestigial model is permitted to live on.

When cases like Amtrak build up and contribute to government expenditure, yearly taxes from citizens may not be enough. The response to this from the government is to extend the supply of money, by inflation and debasement from the monetary standard. This directly harms the foundation of liquidity, which as discussed can fuel demand for authoritarian rule as in the Weimar Republic.

These two offshoots of Penn Central show the limitations of governmental established-determination very well. It also shows the resourceful potential of privatized self-determination.

Once again, it is of utmost importance to note that while these societal systems are binary in their purest form, they are rarely ever pure. A communist or capitalist society may either be libertarian or authoritarian.

An example of a libertarian communist society could be loosely likened to that of independent Catalonia:

- A pseudo-socialist society that shares its spoils among the population, this society has few (or no) biases regarding race, ethnicity, religion, or sexuality. While consent to the actions of the state are implied, there is no harsh penalty for having political dissent or using the public forum for a political purpose. Rather than a single, powerful central government there are multiple independent republics.

Compare this to the authoritarian communists of the Soviet Union under Joseph Stalin:

- An absolutist socialism that uses government acquisition to distribute spoils to the population, this system has rigid guidelines for what is permissible religiously, ethnically, and sexually. Consent to the actions of the state are non-negotiable, and harsh penalties may follow political dissent or improper use of the public forum. There is a single, unified central government that oversees all economic facets.

For capitalists the same is true. While fascist governance has some form of socialism, entities like Mussolini's Italy could be considered an authoritarian capitalist state:

- A nation with an open economy, that allowed for upward mobility as well as market diversity. However, loyalty to the state wasn't to be questioned as the country itself was consumed by nationalism. There were severe limitations upon use of the public forum, suppression of secularism, and a consolidated position of power with no political pluralism. The spoils of the open market were meant to serve only those of Italian nationality.

The rules change for libertarian capitalism:

- This would be a country that also utilized open economic contributions. While this market is open, there are no preconceived notions against varied uses of public forums, political pluralism, or secularism. Governmental roles are limited as power becomes less consolidated and the private sector expands; far beyond the point permissible under authoritarian rule. The downside to this is a lessened focus upon domestic economy and national autonomy.

Communism and capitalism are dueling methods of achieving the best societal structure. While one seeks to achieve this via a united strategy of market, the other aims for market diversity.

Expectedly, purified forms of these governments suffer from intense backlash. Rallying an entire population behind such specific margins is nearly impossible, especially if the nation considered is extremely secular.

The only margin that is realistic in the long term is a marriage of both ideologies: using capitalism to promote development, and a socialist government practice to help maintain a bottom line socioeconomically. A consideration for this balance is preserving national autonomy from rogue capitalist influence while also protecting the intrinsic worth of liquidity and self-determination from communist influence. Any deviation from these components leads to zealous nationalist backlash, out of which authoritarian rule can manifest.

Democratic Republicanism, State Capitalism

The pure forms of communism and capitalism serve as ideological concepts more so than actual practices. While semi-pure incarnations of communism have existed to an extent, the sheer size of modern societies seems to only allow these experiments to end in hierarchical despotism. As stated before, fast evolution from agrarian societies into industrial communism has proven difficult; a concept addressed by Marx in 'Capital Volume I'.

Capitalism also has not experienced a purified form in the modern world. Each instance of unmitigated capitalism has been accompanied by government checks and balances, amounting to a degree of socialist practice. This is to the ultimate benefit of sovereign nations as a whole, given that capitalist ideology beholds profit above regional loyalty. Without a system in place to curb profit-driven rule, opportunistic human nature would give way to the privatized vampiric treatment of nations across the world.

The ultimatum stated above also has its own incongruence. The mutt societies that have come from capitalism have shown as much promise as they have dystopia. The modern world has globalized its economic operation, making capitalism the predominant template. It becomes of increasing importance to study the variations of these models in order to refine their operation, with the assumption that some sort of socialist bottom line is the permissible role of government oversight. To avoid bureaucracy this role should be as small as possible, lest overreaching state power begins to compromise self-determination.

Regardless of opinion or personal biases capitalism seems to be the trend of globalized integration, so it will be under these terms that the system must be improved.

Each of the following offshoots of capitalism can be well understood simply by their etymology.

Democratic republicanism refers to a united group of republics, wherein democratic elections provide officials to represent the will of the citizens. These republics may have some sort of macro-federal oversight, but as per their name they are meant to have their own self-determinative status in most matters of policy.

State capitalism is a creation where state-affiliated companies take on roles of political influence based on their efficacy in capitalist markets. In other words, dominant industries have the ability to persuade government action through fiscal coercion of state officials. This overrides any union of republics and relinquishes policy to the will of the most successful capitalist companies.

Just as it may seem, these two systems contradict each other. For a democracy to work, the will of the people must be the primary means of political operation. Industrial or market-based political influence diminishes the relevance of voter self-determination. Under such conditions the even playing field of democracy becomes a two-tiered system, permitting the will of industry to come first and the will of the people to come second.

The inflation of industrial influence on social policy also has a compounding effect on any federal government, siphoning more money into its operation and expanding its role into dense bureaucracy.

Democratic republicanism, much like the Catalonian libertarianism, has only existed in brief stints. Yet it is an experiment filled with promise. The initial concept behind the United States was that of democratic republicanism; even the name *United States* suggests as much. Constitutionally it is implied that the will of the individual states would be held sacred above much federal oversight. While Federalists like Alexander Hamilton and George Washington levied for a more powerful federal government, figures like James Madison and Thomas Jefferson campaigned for focus on Republican self-determination.

It is an interesting note that the etymology of the current political parties in the USA have morphed into "Democrats" and "Republicans" given that their origins were birthed from the same place. In the infancy of the United States the bipartisan parties were Democratic Republicans and Federalists, butting heads over the size and role of the federal government.

When American republics had more autonomy they were permitted to do such things as regulate their own legality of products, print their own currencies, and subsidize or eliminate their own industrial markets. This added a unique extension to the capitalist paradigm, further expanding on the core concept of market diversity. The more decentralized regional structures of power are, the more difficult it becomes for sordid outside influence to pollute democratic process. Prospectively the only role of federal oversight was a small means of socialism to ensure a bottom line of life quality, provide measures of security against foreign powers, and protect public forum/private rights via constitutional law.

Theoretically speaking this all sounds quite functional. Yet the democratic republicanism of the United States has hardly progressed from that established by the ancient Greeks. Only Caucasian males over a certain age were allowed to participate in democratic process. Blacks, women, natives, and other marginalized peoples were excluded from the "equality" advertised, making state affairs preferential to a race- and gender-based hierarchy. The USA being secular from its outset would have needed to include these margins to create democracy, and in falling short of this built upon a cracked foundation for true democratic republicanism.

Aside from sheer lack of progressivism, the reasons behind the exclusion of African-Americans and Native Americans from democratic process were truly dehumanizing. Conceptually, the first generations in United States citizens saw a need for financial capital in their new country. This was in part to resolve debts from the Revolutionary War, but was also required to create a higher international standing economically against other nations that had existed for hundreds or thousands of years. To do this the widespread practice of slave labor was permitted to exist, so that the economic spoils of the nation's primary labor industries could be siphoned into building the international standing of the United States. For natives, the reason against democratic participation would be that the lands kept by tribes were to be sovereign nations all by themselves. As these nations were not part of the USA, their constituent peoples could not technically vote.

An underlying concern beyond this was that the US likely always knew there would be degrees of expansionism into Native American territory. Allowing a democratic voice to the natives could hinder this process. Even after the dissolution of the majority of their nations, Native Americans were excluded from democratic participation until 1962.

In its prideful democratic infancy, the United States had limited its scope of equality so severely that the great experiment was impossible to use as reference for true democratic republicanism.

That being said, the nature of democratic republicanism innately staves off authoritarian leanings and holds high promise of libertarian leanings. Save for overreaching federal oversight that may usher in authoritarian rule, independent republics are small and manageable enough to ensure against monopolization of power or economy. The only modern reality that could be problematic in a democratic republic is that foreign nations may use the lessened federal power as means for invasion. No doubt, the largest socialized program needed federally in a democratic republic would be that of the military.

Giving authority of republics over their respective federal entity could curb misuse of military strength. This could occur by eliminating benign or sordid agencies on the federal level, and permitting republic-based oversight of the national military. Coupled with libertarian social outlooks and economic practice this civil structure may have unprecedented potential.

Expanding upon the economic implication of a democratic republic is its state of liquidity. Under the Articles of Confederation in the United States, republics and individual banks were allowed to print their own currency until ratification of the Constitution. This happened again following the Civil War, ending with the establishment of the Federal Reserve in 1913. With so many types of currencies available, a two-fold discussion could be made.

Without a monopolized currency there is little means to create debased (or fiat) monies. The intrinsic worth of a person's money can be linked to constant international standards like gold or silver, regardless of their value fluctuation. Overspending by the federal government is far more difficult with multiple currencies, and the ability for capitalist sink or swim rhetoric is able to function in the market of money. Currencies that perform poorly die off, and successful ones gain a dominant foothold.

As one may assume though, this has savage implications.

Should a bank or republic issue a poorly performing currency that defaults, all of the holders of that money are at serious risk. As with other capitalist industries, it becomes the job of the consumer to keep tabs on their choice of money and refrain from passive involvement. For the system to work and keep collateral damage low, its constituents must be active and analytical in their choice of currency. This isn't terribly different from international currency hedging, forex trading, or exchange rate monitoring.

An alternative to this system is the current US standard: a single unified currency that is easily debased, manipulated, wasted, and yields interest to a select few in charge of the currency market. Furthermore, the inflationary nature of the singular fiat dollar augments federal expansionism and is not redeemable to a standard.

The populace must be educated and active enough to fulfill their own self-determination regarding money; otherwise monopolized structures will gladly appear to do the job for them.

A series of united republics could very well change the global paradigm of governance, provided all individuals are addressed as equals and the federal level is subservient to its parts. Perhaps if the United States had allowed the former, the latter would have been assured. This consideration is speculative at best, but is invaluable to help shed light on future phases of political experimentation.

State capitalism has roots in many governmental archetypes. As mentioned in the discussion of liquidity, liquid exchange allowed for individuals and businesses to have a new dispersal of power at their fingertips. This in turn makes the balance of social power shift to those who have access to large amounts of capital, regardless of whether they historically had to share that power with a monarch, dictator, or republic. As prominence of industry began to determine international standing, the importance of nations retaining good ties with powerful businesses became of extreme importance. This reality only grew under the industrial and technological revolutions.

The resulting hierarchy was one that placed the relationship between industry and government above the relationship of government and its constituents. Even though the people are the driving force behind production and demand, globalized markets could assure that in the modern age those prerequisites could be met overseas if a domestic government were too restrictive on industry. A nation could very well shoot itself in the foot economically should it tread too heavily upon the gears of major business.

The preferential treatment implied also has tremendous effects regarding the free market advertised in traditional capitalist ideals. Were a singular private business to become powerful enough of an influence over governmental practice, it could use policy to eliminate competition in the market and create a monopoly.

The most impactful instance of this relates back to free market of currencies.

Homogenization of currency took effect in the United States circa 1913 as the Federal Reserve, the third central bank of America, unified all monies into the US dollar. After the Civil War the markets of currency and banking institutions were extremely diversified, along with accompanying industrial and technological revolutions. As private business expanded beyond all previous precedents, citizens after the American dream had a multitude of entities to shop from for loans, competitive savings accounts, and investment opportunities. This immense market made prominent banking institutions and industrialists nervous, in particular J. P. Morgan, the Rockefeller family, the Vanderbilts, and Kuhn Loeb & Co., amongst a few others.

With their accumulated influence over state affairs these figures were able to create a centralized bank of the United States. Meeting on Jekyll Island off the coast of Georgia this coalition of aristocrats sought to monopolize currency, push smaller banks out of business using government legislation, and effectively make their own companies immune from bankruptcy via government subsidy. All of this came to be in a relatively short amount of time, as the budding plethora of US banking and currency options dwindled under the scrutiny of the newly established Federal Reserve System.

Using their extreme influence over state affairs and the pretense of resolving World War I debt, a select few entities were able to circumvent the ideals of traditional capitalism and replace them with state capitalism, a thinly veiled chameleon of its cousin.

It wasn't destined to stop there. Following in the footsteps of other great empires such as Rome, industrial control of government has little concern for the personal sanctity of a nation's populace. The resulting policies essentially use the credit and debt of a nation to enrich the privatized powers that be. This extends to all government functions, often using moral debt or red herring rhetoric to report back to the public's curiosities on spending.

This practice only grows with former private business executives and lobbyists moving their role directly into politics.

Four examples can be observed:

1. For the unfortunate reality of war, privatized influence sanctions a neo-imperialist practice. A nation can be goaded into wars for the purpose of resource acquisition, diplomatic coercion, regional control for trade, or any personal reason. Put simply, the military, its manpower, and its technology are at the whim of the highest bidder. Often this will be the whims of many private entities, drawing manpower from a variety of governmental organizations or private security firms. Selling these wars to the population becomes a simple matter of advertising, the use of moral debt to convince a nation that their values must be spread, the threat of national safety, or the promise of a better future for the country being invaded.

2. For economics this would mean that state and international trade deals would cater to the growth of capital for state capitalist companies rather than the benefit of any national autonomy. Protective tariffs, trade deficits, and domestic job markets all become of little concern. The goal of trade agreements brokered between major industry and government is to maximize profit and lower overhead, putting product safety, human rights, national economies, long-term sustainability, and market diversity in the firing line. These trade deals are often met with a favorable response by the public as some imported products may come at a lessened price, having been made overseas. But the action-reaction is a serious threat to the free market, traditional capitalism, and the principles of a democratic republic.

3. The environmental and human rights concerns applicable to traditional capitalism are inflated when compounded with state capitalism. Consider a natural resource like water. In the

western United States drought is a consistent issue, making natural sources of water an invaluable resource. If left solely to the operations of government it is reasonable to think that there may be a way to distribute this resource fairly, provided there is oversight from the civil planning and scientific communities. Yet in the state capitalist model this prospect cannot exist. Through a capital-based hierarchy, a private company can buy rights to land with water—and monopolize the resources held there.

This is a reality in Northern California during drought season, as corporate monolith Nestlé bottles precious water and sells it back to the populace with no regard for the basic needs of the Californian people. To emphasize the impact, Nestlé pays under $600 a year for its pipeline permit costs. This is likely due to Nestlé's state capitalist influence over the Californian government. Summarizing, a necessary resource is monopolized at cost to the public while permit revenue is dodged, cheating taxpayers of both water and permit capital that could contribute to Californian infrastructure.

4. The impact of state capitalism also has counterproductive effects on socialism. The basic social purpose of government becomes a boon to private industry more so than to the people. By allowing corporate influence over socialized funds, these funds become a piggy bank for private gains.

Social Security in the USA is a prime specimen, as the supposedly guaranteed trust fund has been used for general government expenses with very little realistic compensation. Namely, the government is supposed to repay social security borrowing with interest to the trust through guaranteed bonds- but those hypothetical repayments will also come from taxpayer money. This essentially means that social security is paid for in taxes, borrowed from to fund a myriad of government endeavors, then will be paid for *again* in taxes. This model all but assures that insolvency will occur, though it will be delayed as long as possible via deference of bond redemptions.

In a nutshell, the social security program is funded by taxation, which is then borrowed and subject to taxation.

These misuses of government power by state capitalist entities rely on complicit advertising in media outlets. These outlets are homogenized in the same fashion as banking or insurance. By virtue of state capitalist influence, conservative and liberal margins can be preset for civilian discussion without giving insight into the true practice of government. While this is so subversive that it may even seem like hyperbole, it is important to keep in mind that the public forum must at least appear to be open lest the historical model of repression-revolution be repeated. Some measure of dissent and opinion must be allowed to continue for state capitalism to operate under the veil of a democracy. The margins of discussion and dissent, however, are kept under surveillance.

It goes without saying that all of these private aims become incredibly expensive for a government to maintain. Eventually money under such duress will become spread so thin to its standard that it becomes intrinsically worthless. If too much money is printed or credited that it is only worth a minuscule amount of gold, it becomes functionally worthless on the international market and must be de-standardized. Expectedly this happened in the United States and the US dollar became irredeemable to a gold standard circa 1971.

Likely it was directly due to state capitalist expenditure that a standardized currency could not continue to be used in the United States. Most certainly not after the US dollar became World Reserve currency for growing nations to borrow (not coincidentally soon after the removal of the gold standard).

The contrast between state capitalism and democratic republicanism is actually more at odds than capitalism and communism. While a capitalist society can have pseudo-socialist elements to its government function, the very theme of state capitalism contradicts democratic republicanism. As contrasting systems, these two are likely the closest to binary. If the voice of industry is permitted above that of the people, a democracy cannot truly exist. Similarly, if the voice of the people is raised above that of industry state capitalism cannot exist.

State capitalism in the modern age operates behind the scenes of other political forms. As these business entities are by nature multinational, they are not beholden to the countries in which they operate. Rather the reciprocal—the countries that permit their presence are beholden to them.

Anarchy, Theocracy

The final contrast of governmental systems addresses a futuristic potential and an antiquated bludgeon. Upon further examination of self-determination and established-determination, an inevitable roadblock comes into sight. The presence of a deity or a higher being is a deeply laid facet in the lives of so many people; when addressing government and morality how can belief be ignored?

In short, it can't.

The presence of belief has been a pivotal landmark for so many civilizations, it has defined nationality, ethnicity, and morality. The moral debt of religion has been a recurring theme in war and imperialism as well. Depending on the belief system (deistic or not) there is a defined amount of established-determination that accompanies credence. A higher being is often referenced for a code of conduct, and much like the state monopoly of force a certain pluralism must be removed for belief-based piousness.

Before delving into anarchic and theocratic dissection, a frame for religion must be made. The dogma related to religious beliefs has driven many significant events throughout history. The Inquisitions to the Roman Empire, the Ottoman Empire, and the regional variations of Christianity brought on by Martin Luther all had significant geopolitical ties. This reality is so defined that world governments have often sought to appease religious entities so as to garner the support of their followers.

A powerful instance would be the tax exemption of religious institutions by various governments, and the expectation of a tax base to be provided without these megalithic groups.

In World War II another excellent example took place. As the Nazi Empire spread south, it became accustomed to the practice of claiming a nation's precious metals and valuables as its own. The prospect of this scared the Vatican so badly that the Catholic Church offered its endorsement to the Reich. This decision was made so that the church need not worry about the Nazis commandeering the vast riches underneath Vatican City. In exchange Germany would have the official backing of the Catholic faith, a truly gigantic population base worldwide.

The power behind faith is a driving force of political ideology, even in secular nations. The clear-cut fundamentalism of extreme religious zeal makes for a moral code that can't reconcile with other beliefs, creating religious governments that have killed countless individuals in order to "save" them in the next life.

This is by no means limited to deistic belief systems. Atheist leaders such as Stalin and Pol Pot essentially treated their statism as a deity, and no other belief system was tolerated. By some measure, this practice ended no differently than religious fundamentalism.

For all intents and purposes the definition of *theocracy* will be "a state governed by a belief system, with or without a deity." This core belief system serves as an absolute control, with no rotation of power. In such a system the faces of rulers may change, but the underlying conduct and dogma does not.

The preconceived concept of anarchy must also be redefined. Following in the footsteps of David Graeber and Noam Chomsky, the status quo definition of anarchy is far removed from its real political potential.

When the word *anarchy* comes to mind it conjures images of a world in flames, a removal of all development and social progress from the human race. Molotov cocktails and falling planes enter the mind's eye, as all forms of monopolized power fail to limit interpersonal pluralism, allowing the most nefarious of human nature to surface. But this definition is extremely limited in scope. The functional, political definition serves as a more thought-provoking subject: *"absence or denial of any authority or established order"* (Merriam-Webster, 2017).

Alternatively: *"anarchy is the condition of a society, entity, group of people, or a single person that rejects hierarchy."*

A denial of established authority or hierarchy may not mean the abolition of government or social workings. Rather it could be interpreted as the continuous removal of entrenched power, a perpetual cycling of power-based roles, that occurs with enough frequency that no hierarchy can reasonably take permanent hold.

One could argue that the idea of implementing term limits to government offices is not just a libertarian principle, but also anarchist. So long as power is only held in the short term and removed completely, anarchists surmise that oppressive authority can't take hold.

The only remaining hierarchy to be addressed is that of education. Should this cycling of power be possible, it would rely on the majority of the population being educated enough to be involved in political and economic action, as well as civil or social works.

Established educational hierarchy limits the spectrum of individuals that can hold office to an upper echelon of aristocrats. With little education regarding political affairs in lower class schooling, much of the world's population can't afford to learn about these subjects in college, don't realize they may have interest in them, or find them so intimidating that they choose to let others lead.

The level of self-determination needed for an anarchist society is even more demanding than that of responsible capitalism. Education must be reformed for perpetual power cycling, yet the entrenched powers of government control public education.

It is the institutional equivalent of asking a man to shoot himself in the foot.

In this hypothetical idea, however, it would seem impossible for theocratic dogma to take root. Especially in the widening secular world, the recycling of people in positions of authority could offer an even keel of ideas and democratic action. While long-term societal projects may have a more difficult time developing in government, advocates of anarchy may pose that allowing voluntaristic interaction could compensate.

Regardless of these speculations, it is an ultimate reality that theocratic governance is a residual system of a time long passed. The imposition of specific beliefs on a secular nation (and world) isn't just immoral itself, but implausible. Due to globalization the sheer amount of interpersonal alienation implied wouldn't just stunt the economy; it would cause severe unrest worldwide. Lingering modern theocracies face intense domestic dysfunction.

Saudi Arabia has a Sunni Muslim theocracy, following a strict doctrine of Sharia law. Under this set of ordinances other faiths are forbidden, women are treated as second-class citizens, consumption of goods like alcohol are outlawed, media is heavily suppressed, and personal relationships are heavily monitored. This accompanies a draconian level of punishment for petty crimes including limb amputation and capital punishment, boasting the third highest rate recorded of execution in the world next to Iran (another theocracy), and China (a statist regime). There are very few records provided for war-torn nations like Syria or hermit nations like North Korea.

For Saudi Arabia this theocratic rule is accompanied by a staunch monarchy led by the Al-Saud family, who sits atop a dramatic class hierarchy. The rules of Sharia law do not apply to the monarchy, as drinking, personal freedoms, and hedonistic pleasures are enjoyed by the ruling class. The working class no doubt breeds dissent toward their royalty, yet this is deflected by state-sponsored anti-Western sentiments.

Despite the Saudi government working closely with United States and Israeli interests, they heavily subsidize Islamic fundamentalism, whose rhetoric is aimed voraciously against Western hegemony. By fostering the image of an enemy outside of the state itself, Saudi Arabia deflects its citizens' concerns away from the royal family. By no coincidence this is coupled with one of the highest government arms acquisitions in the world, a scenario that likely shows the monarchy stocking up for social unrest.

Ex-CIA operative Robert Baer has the following quotes from his book *Sleeping with the Devil* (2004):

> *The Saudi government probably spends more per capita than any other country in the world on arms. (It acknowledges only that it spends 13 percent of its gross domestic product, but half of its revenue is earmarked for the military).*

> *Anger against the West and particularly the United States spills all over the Land of Islam. But there are groups that all the signs keep pointing to—the Wahhabis, the Muslim Brotherhood, and al Qaeda, of*

*course—and there's one place that serves more than
any other as the principal backer: Saudi Arabia.*

*Things are even worse than they seem. Saudi Arabia
doesn't have what we would call a rule of law. Look
inside a Saudi passport: It states that the holder
"belongs" to the royal family. A Saudi commoner is
chattel, a piece of property no different from an Al
Sa'ud's Jeddah palace or his Rolls-Royce Silver Cloud.*

Two interesting points can be speculated upon.

One is the glaring US alliance with the Saudis, a partnership
that screams hypocrisy given the royal family's suppression of
freedom and condoning of extremist factions. This simply comes down
to US state capitalist interests sharing their goals with the family
Al-Saud.

For the US an alliance with the Saudis means better-priced oil
exports and a cohort in the Middle East that can help edge out
competing oil nations like Iraq, Syria, or Iran. For the Saudis it means
cheaper munition imports and an assurance that the US will not
invade, as well as a better preparedness for their own eventual
domestic unrest.

The other point is a philosophical question to be had regarding
theocracy. Clearly with their lavish conduct, the royal family is not
subject to the rule of belief that they impose upon their people. Were
the deity of Islam to be as strict as Sharia law suggests, His laws
would have to be followed by the Al-Saud. Then the question becomes
not one of religious devoutness, but one of purpose:

Is a potential purpose of theocracy not to serve belief, but rather aid in perpetuating hierarchy?

Could the moral, dogmatic, and societal debt of belief be used as a simple mechanism to subjugate the Saudi masses? If so, it would only make sense that the upper aristocracy would fund and push these beliefs to thicken the moral veil.

Another interesting study focuses on the Theravada Buddhists of Burma and the indigenous Rohingya Muslim population.

Much like Saudi Arabia, Burma (Myanmar) is ruled by a privileged class. Instead of a monarchy, it is an exclusively Buddhist military junta. While Burmese citizens exist in economic despair (one of the twenty poorest nations in the world according to the UN) the junta lives as a state within a state, existing in literal immunity from the realities of their nation. Given the nature of this military rule there is a severe monopoly of power and limitation of the public forum. These factors coupled with the intense poverty of Burma yield extreme nationalist sentiment that requires an outlet, and the junta state must channel such criticism away from itself.

The chosen means of this deflection is to focus dissent toward the marginalized Muslim Rohingya, a disenfranchised and unpopular people due to their faith and minority status. As they do not coincide with the ethnic and theocratic narrative of larger Burma, the Rohingya are stateless; unclaimed as people by the Burmese government and subject to internment in work camps, execution, and deportation. Pushing a view of Rohingya Muslims as "savages," "heathens," and a destructive force to the Burmese economy, the junta is able to dissuade criticism from its own government.

Belief is a serious facet to this, as the Theravada majority is used as a means of unity to incite and justify group action. As the years have progressed, this situation has come under international scrutiny, and democratic measures are slowly being taken. It's interesting to see the international community pushing for reform with a small nation like Burma while being much more complicit with the questionable conduct of a large and economically invaluable nation like Saudi Arabia.

The value of morality doesn't always supersede the value of economics, it would seem.

For many nations theocracy provides safe haven for other deep-seated prejudices. In many African nations homosexuality has been viewed as unforgivable, exacting judicial repercussions as terrible as incarceration and execution. Over thirty African countries have made homosexuality illegal. This sentiment has pervaded many African cultures peripherally, but was reinforced by the colonial imposition of Christianity.

While many indigenous African cultures were at odds with homosexuality originally, the safe haven of extremist Christian beliefs has allowed for these sentiments to expand and exist well into the present. Armed with the backing of religious dogma, many budding African nations are able to justify the continued repression of sexuality.

This sort of established-determinism pulls focus away from the true concerns that should be had for developing nations—such as economic growth, improving development, the public forum, liquid stability, and security from separatist factions. By emphasizing the witch hunt for a marginalized group, developing nations drive a wedge between their own citizens while simultaneously delaying their progress toward national autonomy.

While many of these countries are not technically Christian nations, they have an element of theocratic pretense that serves to the detriment of their standing in the global community.

The same criticism can be applied in the United States. While the initial ideal of religious freedom has been a hallmark in the history of the USA, there have always been preferential undertones of theocracy. Religious institutions are exempt from taxation (an industry of approximately $1.2 trillion a year according to one Georgetown study, more than Apple and Google combined).

Many people in a secular nation like the USA are agnostic, atheist, or do not follow conventional religion. Their tax dollars still help to prop up the mega belief engine that only aligns with a section of the populace. Even aside from this, the United States has always been predisposed to a Christian majority that pervades the political arena.

An interesting occurrence can be seen on the US dollar, sporting the phrase *In God We Trust*. This didn't actually appear on the US banknote until 1956, until after the Cold War had begun. *E pluribus unum* (out of many, one) had been the previous unofficial motto of the US, but as the threat of the "godless communists" of Soviet Russia grew Americans developed a renewed piousness for monotheism. The unity of a deistic belief was meant to help combat the Soviet heathenism, an age-old political soapbox reminiscent of the Crusades.

The appearance of the same phrase upon coinage had occurred in 1864 after religious petition to essentially state that God was on the side of the Union during the Civil War. In the "Star Spangled Banner" by Francis Scott Key, "In God Is Our Trust" is recited. His commission of this musical piece coincided with the War of 1812, where the British actually took Washington, DC.

From this it would seem another observation about theocracy can be made. Times of war and economic stress provide entry to belief-based power structuring. Be it deistic or atheistic, a primary way to reassure and pacify the masses is to reference a higher purpose or power.

Should there be a guiding light of god, state unity, or both, the sharp blows of war or recession can be softened seemingly. The use of belief once again appears to be aimed at maintaining order and complicity within a national narrative. To further the concept, it must always be considered that nations are at war with each other's values and morals. Even allies compare their society to others based upon moral action, and the placating of the religious majority is an excellent way to assure good faith in government amongst the masses.

It must be emphasized: while theocracy lacks tangible benefit for the people, that does not mean that belief systems themselves are to be dismissed. Culture, ethics, history, and much more are preserved in belief. Belief also inspires many people to build positive personal relationships and even expand upon societal development. For global secularism to continue its upward climb belief systems are integral, as is acceptance of all their incarnations.

However the preservation of power structures and political dogma based on belief systems must not persist in the future.

The antithesis of theocracy demands a constant removal and restructuring of power. Rather than a steadfast and definite rule of law centered around belief, the anarchist aims to remove entrenched power as often as possible so as to prevent rigid hierarchy. The centerpiece to this movement would be the addition of educational systems to the public forum. Just as the public forum is meant to widen debate on economics, policy, and sociology, so too would the systems of education need to address these subjects. Additionally, educational institutions would have to permit open discussion of the aforementioned.

Formal educational outlets have a tendency to either gloss over civil subjects or push an established-determinative narrative. Even in higher collegiate education it is not uncommon to find sympathetic rhetoric toward monetary inflation, historical imperialism, or state capitalist economics. For anarchic power cycling to work properly a wide base of opinion and education would be needed, without the limitations of conventional schooling.

In a way this would promote an extreme democracy, where constituents would have to be perpetually involved in government affairs. Constant elections or representative replacement would have to be reinforced by an active and engaged populace. Another caveat could be the removal of preferential treatment toward government officials, state capitalist companies, and belief institutions.

With an extremely temporary position, representatives would also be subject to a curbing of hierarchical practices such as post-tenure pensions, above median income pay, or lobbying.

Notes

Each set of these governmental structures subsists as an impure form. Burma is an authoritarian theocracy that is working to embrace democratic republicanism. Canada is a libertarian state capitalistic nation with left leaning socialistic programs. Israel is a democratic republic that operates under loose theocracy, riding the line between libertarian and authoritarian for different marginalized groups. Iran is an authoritarian theocracy with state capitalist ties. The United States is a state capitalist nation with theocratic undertones, thinly rebranded as a democratic republic.

These eight terms are meant to give landmarks for insight into the characteristics of governmental and societal evolution. The great experiment of civilization is not unlike experimentations in chemistry, finding compounds that work together and hopefully learning which combinations are deadly.

The only system that is truly detrimental to global growth is the system that is not understood by its people. Without the understanding of historical context or political philosophy, political evolutions are destined to repeat.

The twentieth century brought an end to a predominantly monarchic world. Political curiosities amassed as a result of globalization, as well as technological and industrial revolutions. What was to follow would be a century of societal experimentation and combative ideologies, many of which had little time to gain the foothold needed to prove their effectiveness.

To understand and analyze a national structure, the four foundations and their accompanying governmental structures must be viewed in tandem. Often the foundations serve as a way to see into the future of a nation as they reshape under governmental structures. It must also be noted that the diversity of a population and its surrounding geography affect these factors.

For Baltic nations there is a high quality of life, supplemented by effective social programs and low domestic violence. Yet this model is achieved easier in nations with homogenous racial and ethnic groups than in a highly secularized country. With a wide variety of cultural, religious, and social norms the role of government must also diversify. This task is often easier said than done—especially when combating entrenched theocratic, authoritarian, or nationalist sentiments.

Geography also creates a curious pretense for political experimentation. The most valuable commodity of civilizations has always been the ability to trade; therefore trade routes or resource-rich lands are coveted. It still stands that nations in the middle of highly valued real estate are subject to global meddling in the affairs of their political evolutions. This can be demonstrated most easily in the turmoil of the Middle East, the Balkan/Zagros/Caucasus Mountains, Central America, or the Fertile Crescent.

As these geographical areas are of extreme trade-related value, larger global powers have sought to control them throughout history. Be it through outright imperialism or a subtler means of control, many geographically integral nations are not left to their own devices to experiment politically; their autonomy is usurped by foreign powers for the use of economic homogeneity.

There is little doubt that the future of the world will be nurtured by a rising dominance of secularity and democracy. But the two must go hand in hand. If supplemented by growth in education and governmental structure this process will be expedited, likely giving a new and promising outlook to the twenty-first century.

Through self-determination the world's nations can likely shed the mantle of global strife, in favor of a new means of coexistence. To embrace this possibility, however, the gears of war must also be deconstructed and studied.

War

I spent thirty-three years and four months in active military service . . . And during that period I spent most of my time as a high-class muscleman for Big Business, for Wall Street, and for the bankers. In short, I was a racketeer, a gangster for capitalism. I helped make Mexico and especially Tampico safe for American oil interests in 1914. I helped make Haiti and Cuba a decent place for the National City Bank boys to collect revenues in. I helped in the raping of half a dozen Central American republics for the benefit of Wall Street. I helped purify Nicaragua for the International Banking House of Brown Brothers in 1902–1912. I brought light to the Dominican Republic for the American sugar interests in 1916. I helped make Honduras right for the American fruit companies in 1903. In China in 1927 I helped see to it that Standard Oil went on its way unmolested. Looking back on it, I might have given Al Capone a few hints. The best he could do was to operate his racket in three districts. I operated on three continents.
—Major General Smedley Butler

The towers are gone now, reduced to bloody rubble, along with all hopes for Peace in Our Time, in the United States or any other country. Make no mistake about it: We are at War now—with somebody—and we will stay at War with that mysterious Enemy for the rest of our lives.
—Hunter S. Thompson

Imagination is the only weapon in the war against reality.
—Lewis Carroll

"Why don't you write an anti-glacier book instead?"
What he meant, of course, was that there would always
be wars, that they were as easy to stop as glaciers. I
believe that too.
—Kurt Vonnegut

Amidst the variations of governmental structure and building upon the four foundations of society, there is the constant pragmatism of conflict. War is always a factor in both the construction and decimation of nations, a Damocles capable of both renewal and condemnation. The pretenses for war (and interpersonal conflict) lie in a bedrock of moral debt, comparative values, reciprocal altruism, and reciprocal antagonism.

With little deviation, national warfare is goaded into being with the pretense of either foundational security or to impose a set of values upon another country. These advertised reasons are hardly the reality for such large-scale dispute.

Just as important as identifying social foundations and governmental structures is the ability to define a national identity. One of the easiest ways to assert identity is to define the antithesis or opposite of what one wishes their identity to be. Through this vice of egoism the act of war can be concealed as more moral or necessary than it truly is.

If an individual considers themselves as generous they will deem the selfish actions of others as inconceivable. Even if they too are subject to selfish behavior, the mental default of calling oneself a generous person will prevent an individual from seeing their own actions in context. Not only does the antithesis help to define identity, but it also helps to protect ego on both a personal and societal level.

Egoism is centric to keeping prevalent power structures intact. A defined narrative of identity is consequently a necessity for prolonged power and policy, helping to limit political pluralism. So long as such justification for violent action goes unabated, warfare can be instated in an assortment of ways. The devices of warfare are not limited to armaments and munitions, but exist also in psychology, economics, and Hegelian dialectics.

As mentioned in the previous section, there is a rift between the actual reasons for war and the reasons advertised to the general populace. This will be a central theme for the following examinations. Trade hubs in particular are hotspots for global conflict, as are key military outposts. The Middle East joins Africa, eastern Europe, the Mediterranean, the Arabian Sea, and Asia, making it a key location for both trade-related and military use. Alliances and wardship over lands in the Middle East yield an advantage globally to those who exercise power over them.

It comes as no surprise that the Suez Canal, Fertile Crescent, Zagros or Balkan Mountains, and North African nations have been subject to many conflicts. Cuba has also dealt with the same yoke as the "Gateway to the Americas." The Founding Fathers of the United States always showed interest in taking Cuba for trade-related reasons, and likely the Spanish occupation of Cuba was a major factor in the Spanish-American War.

A military-related demonstration of these concepts can be found easily through the repeated engagements in Crimea, Ukraine. In the mid-1800s, Russia was at odds with an alliance between France, Britain, and the Ottoman Empire. Russian expansionism was on the rise under the pretense of promoting equality for Orthodox Christians, primarily in Catholic and Muslim lands. To curb the Russian advance, the Allies took Sevastopol in Crimea, one of the only Russian naval ports that functioned year round. This action effectively stopped the war.

To clarify, much of Russia is landlocked. This means that for naval departures there are few options given that the White and other northern seas freeze over for much of the year. The Crimean port in the Black Sea, as well as other naval outposts in Syria and Cuba, are extremely important to the Russian military. If controlled by rivaling powers, this signifies a devastating strategic loss. Modern Cuba has normalized relations with the US, while both Crimea and Syria are in heavy conflict, all during a time when tensions between Russia and the West are high. The former Crimean War provides unique insight into modern geopolitical affairs.

From both the perspectives of trade and military power consolidation, war has shown the potential to become increasingly unpopular in a globalized world. Trade has become a decentralized commodity, and military imperialism a condemnable act in modern rhetoric. The pretenses for war have needed to adjust accordingly in order to garner support from global citizenry. What is most central to these changes are the ways in which war can be committed or incited, as well as the economic boons behind perpetual conflict.

While traditional warfare is easy to recognize, there are more covert ways to disrupt a foreign nation's stability that attracts less criticism from the domestic populace.

Sanctions

When trying to instate "invisible war," sanctioning becomes a key component to the aggressor's arsenal. These policies often enact an embargo upon imports to a nation, an economic barring from global trade, or a limitation to accessible goods and services on the international level. This may include the import of food or medicine, ability to take on international loans, or GDP export to world markets.

There are two implications for large-scale sanctioning.

One is that an international hierarchy must exist. It is more reasonable to consider that a major world power like the United States, European Union, Russia, or China would be able to convince the global community into sanctioning a smaller nation, than the inverse. Uganda would have a much more difficult task forcing sanctions upon the US than vice versa, implying that larger and more economically impactful nations of the world have a larger say in which nations are sanctioned and why. While globalized relations and trade aim to promote a means of equality amongst all nations, they still struggle with this established-determinative quality. Major public forums like the United Nations offer a seat to each of their member nations, yet it still seems that with such things as sanctions there is a heavily tiered scale of national importance.

This brings the discussion to a second point, which is the advertised purpose of sanctioning. A key purpose behind the exclusion and reprimanding of sanctioned countries is supposedly moral in nature. A repressive country with an authoritarian, dictatorial, theocratic, or unstable climate is often in the firing line. International sanctioning is meant to goad a repressive or violent government into progressive action or reform, essentially blackmailing them to initiate a change in policy or government. To make such an ultimatum there must be a moral default that is established by dominant countries that have access to sanctioning others easily. The global standard for morals and etiquette is consequently limited to a select few dominant nations, who then have the ability to impose their will without the use of weapons.

Rather than inspiring an even keel of cultural and systemic discussion, sanctioning often has the ability to stunt sociopolitical growth in developing nations. While the concept of democracy may be foreign to a small developing nation, heavy sanctions can actually cause a dismissive backlash toward the global community as a whole and make the transition toward progressive government into a much longer process. The limiting of essential goods, ability to travel, and general antagonization toward the citizenry of an entire nation can translate into extremist sentiments that often turn zealous.

Such was the story of Iraq in the 1990's under president Bill Clinton and secretary Madeleine Albright.

The story of Iraq's modern relations with the West began after the dissolution of the Ottoman Empire and the subsequent British wardship over its lands. The Middle East was carved up into smaller nations with European owners, each operating with theocratic officials who were loyal to their European wards. From 1932 until 1941 Iraq had a measure of independence, until the British took control of the nation again to assure the safety of their oil lines for use in the Second World War. Even during this short-term independence Iraqis were subject to the presence of many European military bases and personnel.

After the end of the war Iraqi nationalism became extremely popular. The people of Iraq campaigned for autonomy and freedom from the control of international powers. This prompted the rise of a pan-Arabic and secular movement that brought Saddam Hussein to power, meant to combat both international oligarchy and oppressive Sunni theocracy.

It wasn't long before Iran followed suit and ousted their Western installed leader, the shah, with a nationalist revolution that led to Shia theocracy.

It is interesting how Arab nationalism led to a theocratic outcome in Iran and a secular outcome in Iraq, demonstrating how domestic backlash from an oppressive environment can manifest in dramatically different ways.

The revolutionary sentiments in Iraq soon gave way to US and Israeli backing of Saddam Hussein in a war against Iran, wherein chemical weapons were deployed at the Iraqi government's disposal. This situation was aggravated by Kurdish separatists who opposed Iraq, Iran, and Turkey, aiming to create their own state of Kurdistan. This made stability and power decentralization very difficult for the newly independent Iraq—pushing Saddam's government to clamp down on its people to prevent internal revolt and raise measures of security to prevent infiltration by enemy combatants.

A symptom of this rising extremist state was the use of the above-stated chemical weapons. These acts were not condemned regarding their use against Iran, but came under intense international scrutiny when they were used against the Kurds in the chemical attack of Halabja in 1988.

Soon after Iraq's long and bloody war with Iran and the Kurds came the Iraqi invasion of the neighboring state of Kuwait. While advertised as an unprovoked land grab in many media outlets, the Iraqi government was said to be responding to the use of Kuwaiti slant drills which collected oil illegally over the Iraqi border.

Slant drilling allows for the collection of oil over a wide span of landmass, often being capable of siphoning from someone else's land. Saddam approached the international community regarding Kuwait's illegal actions but was met with little recognition. Kuwaiti slant drilling likely threatened one of Iraq's most valuable exports and the sanctity of an independent nation. For this reason Saddam went to war.

Between the Halabja gassing and the invasion of Kuwait a narrative could be constructed to derail any chance of Iraqi autonomy. The new rendition of events could portray Iraq in defiance of the Geneva Protocol against the use of chemical weapons and simultaneously misrepresent the Kuwaiti engagement as acts of aggression by Saddam Hussein.

The purpose of this would be the creation of license for a war against Iraq, to dismantle the Iraqi government and reinstitute international wardship over the nation. By way of moral debt the US was able to garner the support of its own people and international community for a war in Iraq, supposedly meant to protect Kuwaiti and Iraqi citizens from Saddam's tyrannical government. The US offensive would once again make Saddam and the Republican Guard impose measures to further authoritarianism in Iraq, in an effort to maintain control over their splintered country.

A bad taste was left in the mouths of Americans after the Gulf War ended. Saddam had remained in power and countless lives were lost. US army personnel were also poisoned by chemical weapons, many of which were remnants of munitions supplied by Western powers during the Iraq-Iran war. The United States could no longer continue visible engagement with Iraq due to its unpopularity amongst the people. In order to continue waging war a new front had to be made via sanctioning.

The conservative era of Reagan and Bush morphed into a pseudo-progressivism led by president Bill Clinton. Overseas engagements weren't favorable to the American people, but Saddam's government was still painted as morally unacceptable. Granted the Iraqi government had become an extreme authoritarian state due to constant warfare, but it still remained secular unlike nations such as Saudi Arabia. The continued use of moral debt allowed the passive warfare of sanctioning to become the next terrible reality in Iraq.

Beginning during the George H.W. Bush administration, sanctions against Iraq expanded in scope and severity under Clinton and Albright. These included (but were not limited to) a removal of food for oil imports, medicines, water (as Iraq is a landlocked nation), water purification chemicals, and a barring of oil exports out of Iraq.

While the UN expected to allow enough necessity imports to allow civilians their needs, the death toll amounted to hundreds of thousands of children under five years old. Reports of death rates for Iraqi adults during this time vary. The embargo on Iraq arguably had higher mortality implications than traditional warfare, and most certainly had higher rates for young children or infants. When confronted regarding the ramifications of sanctioning Iraq Secretary Albright is quoted saying: *"I think this is a very hard choice, but the price, we think the price is worth it"* (1996).

She later would write that Saddam, not the sanctions, was to blame.

Given this devastating timeline the story of Iraq takes on a new light. After years of war a small and newly independent state had already been forced to implement authoritarian practice. There was not enough domestic stability to begin exploring democratic or self-determinative prospects. The sanctions on Iraq made domestic unrest a permanent reality for Saddam's government. The Iraqi people were without basic necessities, and understandably, many blamed their own government. This made Saddam's authoritarian regime even more extreme. All the while the international community fed this cycle, intervening in Iraqi affairs to stop authoritarianism while ironically augmenting its growth.

The sanctioning of Iraq had the opposite effect than what was desired, if moral nature were the true reason for said sanctions. However, if the objective were to dismantle autonomy in Iraq, sanctioning and perpetual war were quite effective.

Globalization has created a world far more unified than many realize on a day-to-day basis. While worldwide trade has raised the quality of life for an unprecedented number of people, it has also created a model where exclusion from the global marketplace can be more deadly than traditional warfare. It is all too often that such exclusion exists not on the basis of morality, but on the basis of economic compliance. An autonomous state is more expensive and difficult to deal with regarding trade than a state under ward.

As detailed before, the existence of state must be accompanied by some sort of power homogenization. A limit to political pluralism accompanies state-related consolidation of power. The same can be said for morality in the international spectrum. Moral debt and the use of morals or ethics in global affairs are homogenized. The narratives and pluralism regarding these concepts are also limited by the larger players in the arena, as what is and isn't acceptable is determined by stronger military or economic forces.

Therefore a potential even more dangerous than war emerges. When morality and ethics become subjective to a homogeneous power these intrinsic human feelings are easily manipulated or diluted. When the perspective of morality is defined by hierarchy it will almost certainly be used for ulterior motives.

Likely it would be more pertinent to preserve and facilitate infrastructure, including the four foundations, to assist in abolishing authoritarianism. The removal of necessities through sanctioning affects the populace as a whole more so than the higher tiers of authoritarian government, as remaining resources are consolidated for aristocratic use and civil unrest ferments as a result.

Sanctions against Venezuela, North Korea, Russia, Iran, Liberia, Sudan, and many other countries may have probable outcomes similar to Iraq's. Limiting interaction with the global community contributes to established-determination within states, making reform and political evolution difficult to manifest. Revolutionary sentiments increase in likelihood and the state responds with further consolidation of power.

Monetary

Another way to instigate war outside of traditional means is by attacking the liquidity of a nation. The integrity of a nation's money is paramount to its success, both internationally and domestically. With liquidity as well there is an established homogenization to monetary standards. These standards are also set by prominent global powers and kept in check to preserve international hierarchy.

Mediums of liquid exchange have the ability to expand and contract in their value, operating on either a based standard or debased credit. A based standard creates a maximum amount of inflation that can be applied to currency, giving a bottom line for how much deterioration can occur in a currency's value. Debased currencies have no standard and therefore can deteriorate infinitely, as in the case of the Weimar Republic.

The two following case studies illustrate the practice of attacking a nation's currency as means of warfare firstly, and the practice of monopolizing currency as a means to preserve power structures secondly. Without economic stability the means to perpetuate war become non-existent. This has been a significant means of military strategy.

After the fall of Rome there were two fragmented Roman Empires. The Goths, Vandals, Franks, Alamanni, and Saxons were unable to stamp out smaller Roman strongholds; one in western Europe and the other in eastern Europe by the Black Sea. This eastern empire was called the Byzantine and is speculated to be one of the most successful civilizations in ancient history.

Largely attributed to its desirable location bordering the Black Sea and Mediterranean, the Byzantine was possibly the most valuable trade hub in the world during its existence. Constant economic flow gave the architects of this nation the ability to coin an immensely stable currency and collect a rarely fluctuating tax base from Byzantine citizens. The integrity of their money gave the Byzantine Empire a foothold as an economic powerhouse throughout Europe, Asia, and Africa—but its prime real estate also came at a heavy price.

As its location was so desirable, the Byzantine was subject to constant siege from all directions. The Sicilian Empire, Germanic tribes, the peoples of the Rus, Bulgaria, Hungary, the Seljuks of Syria, and many more waged war against the Byzantine Empire. This created a nation facing war at its gates constantly, with ever expanding and contracting borders. The persistent siege of the Byzantine made some citizens disenchanted with their nation, and various civil wars erupted as a result.

But even these factors were not enough to ruin the powerhouse nation of Byzantium, as its economy rested safely in the sheer amount of trade-related industry it was able to provide. The Byzantine currency was standardized, maintaining a definite exchangeable worth during times of economic fluctuation.

Turkish Empires at the time had been waging war at the gates of Byzantine since its conception. The Ottoman Turks in particular were a formidable foe and would be the eventual undoing of the empire, but there was a telltale strategy amongst the enemies of Byzantium. The continuous siege against Eastern Rome had a powerful effect on their liquidity, namely that perpetual wartime spending is unsustainable with a standardized currency. The expenses of paying soldiers and their families, manufacturing weapons, rebuilding infrastructure, and subsidizing food or medicines has an immense effect on the integrity of money.

Despite its megalithic trade economy the Byzantine was forced to eventually debase its currency to facilitate wartime spending, harkening an end to their empire. The removal of precious metal percentages from Byzantine money lessened its intrinsic worth, as goods both domestic and foreign began to cost more. Domestic unrest became more prominent, taxation rose, and infrastructure began to become cheaply made—or not made at all.

There is good speculation that the later Ottoman sieges of the Byzantine in particular were not meant to take land, but to provoke debasement of currency and eventual removal of economic stability. This strategy relies on a nation coming apart at the seams from the inside. So long as pressure is exerted steadily on the borders of a civilization there is little hope for it to cull its spending. For the aggressor nation such a front is relatively inexpensive to maintain, as the goal is not to immediately usurp land or resources.

Inflation and debasement were also factors in the fall of the Old Roman Empire and subsequent Western Roman Empire. Coins that were made of pure silver were reduced to 40 percent silver or 20 percent silver, or debased completely. This rendered them increasingly useless for foreign trade, and the faith of the nation's people in their currency was lost. A key point to this is that liquid mediums are only worth what a society deems them to be worth, so loss of public faith in a medium is a self-fulfilling prophecy. Should the citizenry lose faith in their money, vendors begin to charge more, employment is cut, and economic strife is soon to follow.

Types of currencies that are debased are known as *fiat* monies. They have endless credit potential, but at the cost of their own worth. The more that is created and used, the less valuable it becomes. The undeniable fallout from such spending is economic implosion on a national level; unless there is a larger predefined monopoly of currency in place.

Such a monopoly is the current monetary standard. The hierarchy of nations accepted after 1971 that the debased US dollar would operate as world reserve currency, being lent at interest to developing nations who required capital for infrastructure. The elastic nature of the fiat dollar has helped to cater to the needs of the entire world, as have other fiat currencies: the euro, the pound, the yuan, and the yen. For these funds to be lent so liberally and retain value, there can be no standardized competing currency. A successful nation or trade bloc with gold or silver standardized currency would throw a wrench in the gears of the overinflated fiat market, likely generating troublesome economic upheaval worldwide.

Since the most powerful and economically influential nations have deemed fiat to be acceptable, it is the operating standard for global commerce; barring variations to this design from possibility.

A demonstration of this is shown in the removal of Libya's former leader, Muammar Gaddafi.

Libya was a thriving nation with a high standard of living for most citizens, and modern infrastructure. However, in a similar plight to Iraq's government there were serious authoritarian elements under Gaddafi's rule. These were mostly reactionary responses to constant siege from extremist groups, Egypt, the United States (1986), and various African nations. Early in Gaddafi's career these fronts on Libya committed him to staunch nationalism, a desire to help his own nation develop better security and development. As this desire grew it morphed into a farther extending goal of Pan-Islamic and Pan-African unity, including all-sectarian groups of Muslims and African nations.

Over the years of his rule, Gaddafi started to recognize some very troubling plights in his area of the world.

One was the lack of unity between Muslim nations. Economic demand for oil from the rival denominations of Islam had a way of furthering the divide between African and Middle Eastern nations, making international subjugation of both easier to instate. Western-sponsored nations like Saudi Arabia, Kuwait, the UAE, and Qatar are still at constant odds with secular nations like Iraq, Syria, Egypt, and others. The lack of reciprocal altruism between these nations stood to make fragmentation of the Muslim world a profitable scenario for world powers that wished to usurp their resources. The same can be said for the nations of Africa, whose countries are plagued by internal strife.

The prospect of a unified Africa holds the key to a massive shift in global commerce. Both South America and Africa have been the workhorses for raw materials in global trade, having their resources commandeered for international use over hundreds of years. This design keeps exports as cheap as possible with no environmental oversight, using labor that has little regulation for safety or quality control. The key function to this has relied upon these continents being politically unstable, so that leaders could be installed by foreign governments. Conversely, if a small African or South American nation had a strong nationalist leader, that leader would have to be taken out of power.

Muammar Gaddafi was likely keen to this paradigm; as well he was likely aware of how economically powerful a stable Africa could be. Shifting away from his purely Libyan focus, Gaddafi proposed means to prop up the African world and buck the reigns of international control.

His first proposal was a Pan-African Army. Meant to unify the military power of Africa, this militia would have been meant to drive out insurgents like Al-Nusra and Boko Haram. Consolidating military strength would also have removed the need for interventional actions from NATO or AFRICOM, two agencies that operate under the status quo international hierarchy. The unification of military power throughout Africa could easily render multinational watchdog agencies, who assist in undermining the autonomy of individual nations, benign. Though some African nations also opposed Gaddafi's plan, these concepts are well worth discussion.

The idea of a pan-continental army is also under consideration by the European Union. These bloc armies are not meant to replace national militias; instead they are supposed to augment security over a larger area.

Gaddafi's second idea was to spearhead a Pan-African currency like the euro. Unlike the euro, however, this currency would be based on a gold-backed standard. That being the case all African exports including oil would rise in value, and international compensation for such goods would have a higher cost. Instead of subpar rates of exchange with world powers, a gold-backed Pan-African currency has the ability to permanently change the global model of trade. Not only would it help the nations of Africa stabilize into modern politics, but it could also buck dominant multinational companies from their current economic status.

Circa 2011 Gaddafi's monetary plans were becoming well known in the economic and political world. It is perhaps no coincidence that this timeline aligned with US/NATO intervention in Libya. Under the guise of moral action, international status quo decided unilaterally that Gaddafi's authoritarian government had to be dismantled for the sake of Libyan citizens. Following these actions a well-established and developed state regressed to a war-torn nation in third-world condition.

It is once again thought-provoking that authoritarianism is often the scapegoat for interventionist rhetoric, yet theocratic authoritarianism operates unabated in Western-allied countries such as Saudi Arabia.

Proxy

A final method of covert warfare exists through the means of proxy. A proxy exists as a point between two ends, a middleman, so to speak. If direct engagement in warfare with a powerful nation is unpopular amongst the populace, war can still be waged via other nations with close strategic or economic ties.

The international hierarchy of nations encourages a certain loyalty toward superpower states. For smaller states to operate without threat of invasion or revolution they will often seek a superpower sponsor, to aid them both economically and militarily.

One of the most key examples of a sponsored relationship is between the United States and Israel. Israel, being a relatively new country, was set up in a troublesome situation. During its establishment in 1948 there were harsh colonial means taken against many of the indigenous peoples, and what was to follow would be a difficult path for a budding nation. For various economic, theocratic, racial, and ethnic reasons, Israel was at odds with all of its neighbors. Wars between Israel and Syria, Jordan, Egypt, and Lebanon were vicious and constant.

As all of the nations of the Fertile Crescent were Muslim dominant, there was a fierce loyalty amongst Arab nations to being anti-Western, and many shared the sentient that operating under the economic yoke of the US was insulting. Due to this, many Middle Eastern nations sought the support of Russia to ward off invasion by the American military. The US was at a relative loss for Middle Eastern clients during this time, especially those bordering the Mediterranean in the ever-valuable Fertile Crescent. Having a nation like Israel in the Middle East provided an especially promising opportunity for the US, specifically a stronghold in the Muslim world where Western prospects could be realized.

A synchronized relationship between the two countries began to take shape. Israel would be heavily subsidized by the US in perpetuity and given access to top-of-the-line military technology. Additionally, the United States military would provide support and security measures against other Middle Eastern powers.

In return Israel would hold a key place in the Muslim world for Western trade and development. The Fertile Crescent is arguably one of the most key positions on the globe for military and trade-related purposes. Perhaps unintentionally, Israel was even able to claim and ensure Western use of the Suez Canal after its return to the Egyptian government (1979-1982).

US fiat currency helps to prop Israel up, to the tune of around $30 billion a year in military aid. On a timeline from 1948 this totals over $230 billion, adjusting for inflation. While these figures are approximate they illustrate a very intense desire by the US to retain Israeli confidence.

While there are supposed religious and moral ties for such avid support, the economic implications of having Israel Western-aligned are significant, to say the least. With a key position between Europe, Africa, Asia, the Mediterranean, and connecting Black Seas, Israel (and the Levant) has been a location of desire for thousands of years.

World War II likely would have been much more difficult for Allies on the Western front if it were not for Israel's geographic placement. Even though the state of Israel hadn't yet been formed, Palestine was under British mandate. This meant that oil harvested from the Zagros mountains and fields in modern-day Iraq would be pumped all the way to Haifa in Palestine, for the purposes of fueling

Allied military equipment. There was also a line to Homs in Syria, which had been under French control.

While there was a brief period of occupation in Homs by the Axis powers in 1940, British and free French forces made it a priority to ensure the continued geographical use of Iraq and Syria. They were able to eject the Nazis in 1941. Had the Axis retained control of the Levant, military efficacy on the Western Front would have been stunted severely, leaving Russia and the Eastern Front as the last bastion of focused Allied power.

The Mosul-Haifa pipeline and its Syrian counterpart existed until 1948, when the Iraqi government stopped its flow in protest of the establishment of Israel.

Such is the value of proxy and economic alignment between nations. The emphasis on macro-regional economics in these matters often takes away from the priority of political growth in smaller nations.

In the effort to satiate their superpower sponsors, many growing countries are forced to put national autonomy or public needs on the legislative back burner. This design makes benign power structures, class warfare, and despotism all the more likely.

Referencing the Saudis once more, the structure of Sharia law and the House of Saud are incredibly antiquated systems of politics. While in many nations this oppressive and divisive design would be condemned, US sponsorship sanctions not only the morals of the Saudi government but also its military endeavors. Progressive political growth in Saudi Arabia is impeded by its support from a chosen superpower, and thus has no reason or pressure to change.

Proxy nations can also operate under an installed leadership. If an independent nation refuses to align itself economically with a superpower, it is left open to foreign intervention and potential revolution. Such revolutions can even be sponsored by foreign powers, intelligence agencies, or private security companies that seek to control said independent nation. Once an autonomous nationalist government is removed, the international community is able to install a workable figurehead for their own purposes.

A famous case of such workings existed in Iran before Ayatollah Khomeini. Iran, much like Israel, is at the center of a geographic focal point. It was divided after World War I into separate zones, a British south and Russian north, fueling the Great Game of nations in the early twentieth century. After the end of the war, Iran established a monarchy with a constitution that gave a large degree of national autonomy to the trans-Iranian railway (a massive means of trade) as well as the oil industry.

This government still worked well with its former sponsor states, thus avoiding invasion and installation of a new government. It wasn't until World War II that the Iranian government became a liability to its former ward states.

Despite its neutral status there was a notable Iranian allegiance to Axis powers. The USSR had an intense need for the oil and trade routes in Iran. Citing its neutral status, however, the monarchy wouldn't allow Allied resources to pass through their country. Fearing an eventual alliance with Axis powers, the UK and USSR invaded Iran in 1941. Forcing the hand of the Iranian government made much-needed wartime necessities available on the Eastern Front for Allied use, just as the Fertile Crescent did on the Western Front.

This forced removal of independence left a bad taste in the mouths of the Iranian people and their government.

The monarchy had reasonable concern for permanent land grabs and usurpation of Iranian resources and territories, to which the Allies assured none would occur. However, the gesture of taking over a sovereign and neutral nation by the Allies had created reactionary demand in Iran for nationalist protection. Despite being a sovereign nation, control of the Iranian oil industry was retained by international powers like the United Kingdom. The shah and prime minister of Iran were destined to meet the popular demand for a nationalized Iranian oil industry, so as to remove British cuts from their profits. The response from the British would be a blockade on Iran's trade overseas by the Royal Navy.

This in turn put Iran in a compromising position. National profits fell, the people of Iran became angry at their government, and seeds of a revolution were sown.

The Iranian push for nationalization of their oil industry eventually attracted the attention of the United States, who proceeded to design a coup to overthrow Prime Minister Mossadegh. This consolidation of power to the throne of the shah was accompanied by CIA threats of overthrowing His Majesty as well, if he opposed US interests in the region.

After the coup in 1953 Iran became a ward-state of the USA, having its oil industry controlled and operated by a coalition of multinational companies. History began to repeat, and another nationalist revolution ushered in the rule of Ayatollah Khomeini in 1979.

As seen in this overview, a refusal to comply with large economic or military powers leads easily to the installation of non-democratic governments. Part of this design is the consolidation of power, away from a parliament or other representative positions. Foreign-backed coups undermine political evolution unilaterally, as they rely on established-determination, authoritarianism, and a removal of political pluralism.

Both Iran and Israel exist in these examples as satellites for engagement elsewhere in the world. Be it trade related or for the purposes of war, each state is tied to a superpower.

For other states proxy-related events can further intensify.

Proxy nations can also be a sparring ground for larger world powers. Should two superpowers be hesitant to engage in formal warfare, or if the notion of war is unpopular amongst the citizenry, engagement via proxy nations is a viable option. This is made especially easy given that ward-states often have the above-stated authoritarian degrees to their governance. The operation of such puppet governments can be molded to fit a pretense for war under the guise of moral debt. Once this debt is established a superpower can invade a ward-state of another superpower, unofficially waging war at its doorstep.

A modern proxy war can be observed in the decimated state of Syria. The Syrian government has long been a client of Russia and the former USSR, with a ruling class of officials that are predominantly Shia Alawite Muslims. As one of the nations located in the Fertile Crescent, Syria is much like Israel in its level of value for military and trade use, giving its allegiance powerful leverage in geopolitics.

For Russia such client states are invaluable. The other superpowers of the world (China and the United States) are not as landlocked, having access to a wide degree of accessibility on their coastlines. The Russian landmass, however, is limited in its accessibility, making naval trade and military strategy a difficult endeavor. Throughout history this has been a theme in Russian expansionism. The ability to utilize the geography of smaller countries allows the industrial powerhouse of Russia to match its superpower counterparts in both military and economic capacities.

Syria, Cuba, and the Ukraine are all key players in this concept.

After the fall of the Soviet Union and the dissolution of the Warsaw Pact it was expected by some Russian officials that NATO would disarm as well. NATO was the reciprocal to the Warsaw Pact, having been put in place to stave off the expansionism of the USSR and communist nations. Yet even as the threat of communism fell and the Cold War ended, NATO continued not only to exist, but also to expand. NATO crept closer and closer to Russia. Soon Bulgaria, Poland, the Czech Republic, and a multitude of eastern European nations were poised in NATO alliance. For Russia this would be seen as massively inflammatory, and a direct liability to peace between the Rus and Europe as a whole.

It became imperative that the Russian government retain its ties to former Soviet allies, in the event that a NATO or Pan-European front were to advance on Russian borders. Russian naval units would need to be stationed in former communist states like Vietnam, Cuba, and the Ukraine. The naval base at Tartus in Syria was of arguably even greater importance though, as it offered quick passage to three continents, the Black Sea, and the Atlantic Ocean.

Even though the Cold War was over in theory, NATO expansionism exhibited that if the conditions were right the prospect of war between the West and Russia was still on the table. It would not be until 2011 that obvious proxy warfare began to take effect.

Moving back to Syria, there was a wide disenfranchisement of citizens resulting from the autocratic rule of Alawites. Though Syria was secular, political decisions were limited to a very narrow margin of individuals, all of whom were of a very specific pedigree and creed. This of course resulted in the potential for revolution. The underside of Syria burned with the potential for power upheaval, a potential that was not wasted on the eyes of Russia's rival superpowers.

To advance against Russia covertly, all Western powers would have to do is facilitate the procurement of arms to rebel groups in Syria. This could be easily done and described to Western citizens as a means to confront Syrian authoritarianism without the use of conventional intervention. The veil of this rhetoric operates in twofold, simultaneously using moral debt to justify inflammatory action, while employing saber rattling toward another superpower. Given that conventional war with Russia would be massively unpopular to Western citizens, the method of a Syrian front could disguise the intention as well as the implication.

The United States government would proceed with this plan, arming "moderate rebels" who succeeded in dismantling the Syrian Alawite regime. This had expected fallout, namely the rise of fundamentalist zealotry in the aforementioned rebel groups. The dominance of religious zeal in these factions then prompted the involvement of the Russian military, Iranian funded militias, and eventually a multitude of world powers. The Russian naval base at Tartus is likely compromised as a result of this debacle.

In tandem to this, the Ukraine also became subject to an abrupt and severe disruption of power. Following pro-European Union protests in Kiev, violence erupted in Ukraine that invited an all-out civil war resulting in the removal of the official government. Many claims surfaced that American private security firm Academi was affiliated with training anti-government combatants. Regardless of the validity of these claims the result of the revolution yielded a boon to Western powers.

The newly installed government of Ukraine would be headed by the staunchly nationalist Svoboda party, who would be funded by and defer its government decisions to the United States.

Efforts by the US to prop up the new Ukrainian government had a dual purpose. They would bind the new Ukrainian government to US policy and sabotage bilateral dealings with the Russian Federation, while at the same time targeting another Russian port at Sevastopol in Crimea.

Eastern Ukraine and the port at Crimea managed to remain independent, but it must be considered that the synchronous Western fronts on Ukraine and Syria may not have been coincidental. Shortly after the independence of Eastern Ukraine, accusations of land grabs were aimed at Russia. Not only had proxy warfare hidden the advances on Russia via its clients, but it had also provided license for anti-Russian rhetoric and conventional war in the future.

The collateral damage of proxy warfare is immense and long lasting. In Angola over ten million landmines were deployed during the Cold War in an effort by the Soviet Union to support communist militias. The Angolan Civil War was shadowed by US and Soviet support, exacerbating the already horrific conflict. As fate would have it these mines would not be reclaimed after the end of Angola's war, nor after the Cold War conclusion. They were left in the ground, decimating Angolan civilians for decades to come.

By way of proxy the USSR and US created an independent Angola that would have one of the highest rates of amputations in the world and an astonishing death toll to boot. Figures like Princess

Diana and various NGOs have worked to help in solving this crisis, but the minefields are far reaching and dense.

Alliances, trade blocs, and treaties bind the world into an intensely tribal template. These relationships not only determine global dominances, but they can also set into action a series of domino effects. Should the architects of the international hierarchy use these effects to their own strategic advantage, they could conceivably see far ahead of the average citizen, playing hands that will not be seen for years to come.

Notes

The nature of conflict is far more varied than what is perceived by the general population. It is upon these cruxes that war can be instated passively, or provoked until it manifests actively. Common themes for each of these include economic control, military strategy, and the use of moral debt to garner popular support. A final detail to the nature of warfare in the modern age can be attributed to Major General Smedley Butler of the United States Army:

> *The normal profits of a business concern in the United States are six, eight, ten, and sometimes twelve percent. But war-time profits—ah! That is another matter—twenty, one hundred, three hundred, and even eighteen hundred percent. The sky's the limit.*

The subjugation of smaller nations to their client states doesn't just assure economic dominance of superpowers; it also yields intense profits during actual warfare. State capitalist companies who exert a monopoly on developing nations are contracted in no-bid arrangements to issue weapons to the military, rebuild destroyed infrastructure, and oversee the export of resources after regime changes. As such conflicts assure massive profit margins, it is to the great benefit of many large companies to perpetuate war. This can be endorsed politically through the influence of policy by lobbyists, ex-corporate officials turned politicians, and campaign donations.

For a munitions and aircraft company like Lockheed Martin, there is an added benefit. Lockheed was bailed out of bankruptcy in 1971. The US government deemed the failing of such a company to be a detriment to the economy and American security. As such, Lockheed has operated under heavy state subsidy ever since. This amounts to a business model that is hugely profitable.

The taxpayers fund the capital needed for Lockheed's operation, wars are initiated that require Lockheed's products, the government buys said products with taxpayer money, and the system is repeated. In every rational sense Lockheed receives double profits for its products, footed both times by taxpayer dollars.

The presence of Lockheed Martin lobbyists and ex-officials working as representatives in Washington illustrates a serious conflict of interests. For the average United States citizen perpetual war and convoluted operations of state are an expensive liability. Yet these acts are the bread and butter for privatized industry. The pretense for war must be manufactured as necessary to the public for the paradigm to persist.

The same can be shown in the no-bid contracts given to Halliburton to rebuild the infrastructure of Iraq. These contracts were issued to create usable public works that were destroyed in the war, and also to create new works for the use of the US military. A whopping $39.5 billion has been siphoned to Halliburton subsidiary KBR within a decade. This is in addition to the already lofty government funding of Halliburton's operations, creating the same double profits as seen with Lockheed Martin.

Monopolizing trade and military strategy is certainly a primary goal of warfare and state clientship. Yet there is a more pressing model that becomes increasingly pervasive in the modern world. The multinational nature of a globalized economy emboldens state capitalist companies, allowing their voices to be heard on a level equal to or surpassing that of many nations.

For a nation with no industrial ties, war is only profitable after the conquest of new territories is completed. Purchasing weapons and wartime necessities is expensive, and to an independent government an act that should not be prolonged.

The presence of state capitalist entities in government makes warfare profitable to many. The appeal of perpetual engagement in acts of war becomes a simple means to keep a company's profit margin, and subsidies a means to always have operating capital. Coupled with inflationary currency, a government using this model doesn't care how expensive war may be.

In fact, the more expensive the better—as government priority shifts from fiscal accountability to the taxpayers, to profit accountability to major industry.

This design has expanded since the early twentieth century, coming into shape after the establishment of the Federal Reserve in 1913, and reaching its current model after the destandardization of the US dollar in 1971.

For each of these methods of war to function there must be a divide between state affairs and the will of the people. Moral debt, political or religious dogma, and sponsored xenophobia are all common methods to achieve this.

The need to control public opinion conceivably becomes the most important facet of government, as it supplements power monopolies and limitation of political pluralism. Defined strategies exist to these means, illustrating not only a divide between citizen and government, but also a passive warfare that exists right under the nose of the public.

Operations

In examining the CIA's past and present use of the U.S. media, the Committee finds two reasons for concern. The first is the potential, inherent in covert media operations, for manipulating or incidentally misleading the American public.
—Frank Church

The glory which is built upon a lie soon becomes a most unpleasant incumbrance. . . . How easy it is to make people believe a lie, and how hard it is to undo that work again!
—Mark Twain

There is no part of the executive branch that more exists on the outer edge of executive prerogative than the American intelligence community—the intelligence community, CIA, covert action. My literal responsibility as director of the CIA with regard to covert action was to inform the Congress—not to seek their approval, to inform.
—Former NSA Director Michael Hayden

Secrecy, being an instrument of conspiracy, ought never to be the system of a regular government.
—Jeremy Bentham

Secrecy is the enemy of efficiency, but don't let anyone know it.
—Ric Ocasek

A major theme of the twentieth century has been the merits of representative process, the highest pinnacle of political evolution. While this ideology has been proselytized globally, it has matured alongside economic globalization and the rise of formidable corporate influence in international affairs. This duality has little ability to reconcile. Democracy and representation allude to the promise that every individual has a political voice, yet corporate doctrine alludes to a precedence of industrial-related affairs.

The resulting landscape is a socioeconomic tight-wire for world governments.

Measures of societal and political growth must be shown regularly to the populace, or risk a bucking of the system. Many nations will implement a parliament, extend voting rights to minority groups, permit more libertarian social practices, or subsidize social programs to satiate this public desire. Without controlled development from the state, entrenched power runs the risk of heightened public critique and eventual dismantling.

Without evidence of developmental growth, perceived freedom of public forum, effective liquidity, and a moral bedrock, government will be perceived as ineffective and replaced.

Kin selection and reciprocal altruism in government have become more taboo as society has modernized. This in turn demands a more concealed means of operation for such structures. As outlined in the discussions of subversive warfare, state operations also need to manipulate or avoid public opinion altogether. Achieving such a thing requires psychological influence and intricate insight into how to maintain a hegemonic agenda without full transparency.

Prominence in the global economy has become a defining staple in the order of international hierarchy. National governments who bend to the will of major industry are able to gain a better foothold in the global arena. This must be coupled dually with appeasing a nation's populace and verifying progressive or successful national goals. If a nation excludes international industry it alienates itself from the global economy, effectively sanctioning itself into a likely oblivion. If it excludes its own people a nation is faced with nationalist backlash and eventual revolution.

The modern world is faced with a three-fold paradox: the prominence of national power, the prominence of industrial power, and the prominence of true democratic process. Government must run interference between these three entities, using various operations of state.

Limited Hangout

In 1972 the administration of President Nixon was under heavy political fire. Revelations had come to light that the White House and related organizations had been wiretapping the offices of their political opponents in the upcoming presidential race. Known as the Watergate scandal, these sordid events raised serious questions as to the legitimacy of the president, the US government, and democratic process. Once these actions came to light to the public, a committee was created to look into the issue for the purposes of prosecuting President Nixon.

The following response from the White House exemplifies what is known as a *limited hangout*.

In a last-resort strategy Nixon and his advisors opted to release information regarding Watergate to the investigators. Such information would implicate specific individuals that were involved in the wire-tappings, while sheltering White House involvement. According to the information given by the president and his team, the White House had no knowledge of, or complicity with, the Watergate affairs.

This partial confession served as a limited acknowledgment of Nixon's role in the scandal, meant to appease public demand for the secrets behind Watergate. The investigative committee was appeased for a brief period of time. Even though these events resulted in the impeachment of Nixon, his partial admission of truth was able to conceal a much greater coverup.

The static surrounding the story of Watergate is complex. It gives little insight as to the amount of information retained by the Nixon administration, the potential for a CIA coup using Watergate as license for impeachment, or the true impact against Nixon's presidential opponents.

Said static is the purpose of a limited hangout. By releasing a portion of concealed information, one can refrain from releasing all concealed information. So long as citizens, committees, and the media are free to discuss a partial truth, they don't have to be savvy to a much larger lie. The purpose of limited hangout relates directly to the need for public forum. For a society to remain intact public forum must be perceived as open and free. If parameters for information and discussion are too obvious, the populace will harbor resentment toward their government.

Multiplying the effect of this placebo is the operation of state-sponsored media and controlled opposition. Obsession over released hangout information by the media or political pundits actually helps the purpose of the operation. No matter if these media entities are aware of a limited hangout, their perpetual fixation on the event creates social static.

This makes it nearly impossible for further accurate information to be gathered, much less pressured by the public for release. Severe political critics, loyalists, and experts are all welcomed to the dialogue exchange. The more conflicting voices that can be involved, the better, lowering the curtain to obscure the full scope of the hangout operation.

The presence of dissident individuals and narratives is a key component to a successful hangout campaign. In the effort to manufacture a public forum that appears to be free, there must be critics of entrenched power. While many of these outlets may also be unaware of their place in the operation, they provide an irreplaceable failsafe to the established power structure.

It is through these competing and polarized voices that issues can be supercharged. By supercharging the discussion of a social or political issue, definite parameters of discussion for the issue are further enforced. This has the capability to reduce complex issues into polarized discussions led by a quest for viewers and ratings; or affirmations of personal philosophies, morals, and ego.

Following the analysis of limited hangouts, whistleblowers or leaked information to the public begins to take on shades of gray. Public figures such as NSA defector Edward Snowden, private Chelsea Manning, or WikiLeaks figurehead Julian Assange become subject to a degree of dissonance.

It becomes unclear if the unsolicited release of information through these individuals could be used to spur a discussion that hides the true scope of surveillance, war crimes, or sordid international conduct. Furthermore, if this were the case it would not necessarily imply complicity on the part of these parties. In many ways limited hangout operations are a way to make the best of a difficult situation, giving away some of the gold to preserve the mine.

Another factor in this tangled web is informational sourcing. Much like a children's game of telephone, information has a way of manufacturing its own static through secondary or tertiary sourcing. Depending on the political leanings of informational sources data relayed to the public can be diluted, or redirected altogether. This is particularly relevant in the use of what is known as a *red herring*.

In 2010 private Chelsea Manning (formerly Bradley Manning) was taken into custody for the leaking of classified footage taken in Baghdad. The footage depicted an American airstrike that was initiated against what were thought to be insurgent foot soldiers. Au contraire, the individuals who were attacked were Reuters reporters and civilians. The following controversy created by Manning was meant to address the lack of accuracy in various US military engagements and the implications of widespread collateral damage. This subject came at a time when unmanned drone strikes were being conducted in multiple nations with questionable accuracy, making Private Manning's dialogue extremely pertinent.

Aside from the unneeded tragedy associated with inexact military strikes, these actions have the potential to exacerbate the growth of extremist sentiment and recruitment throughout the developing world.

As the Manning revelations came into the public eye there were mixed reactions. From the standpoint of government and military officials, Manning's leaks were treason in the extreme. They stood to compromise soldiers in the field just as much as they provoked anti-war sentiments, potentially garnering limitations on how and when to engage enemy combatants. A new discussion emerged as to whether Manning was right to expose what she considered to be war crimes.

As large news outlets joined in on the debate the issue no longer reflected a controversy on the use of military power; rather was Chelsea guilty of treason?

This red herring tactic also served to deflect further insight into questionable actions in combat, the use of white phosphorus being a powerful example. So long as the margins of debate stopped at Chelsea Manning and not the content she leaked, the mode of operation for military conduct could be preserved.

Julian Assange, the founder of the infamous WikiLeaks, has been subject to the same sort of distractive red herring. In their absolutely massive catalog of geopolitical exposés, WikiLeaks has given insight into assassination orders, government corruption, war crimes, election tampering, trade agreement meddling, and much more. Many state officials have the same criticism of WikiLeaks as were voiced with Chelsea Manning: that the act of making these things known to the public has the potential to endanger everyday people.

The reaction to Assange's unapologetic leaks was a plan that relied on a defamation of character.

As the international and intelligence community sought to derail Assange, allegations were put underway in Sweden for rape and sexual assault charges against two separate women. In order to avoid arrest Assange took asylum in the Ecuadorian embassy from 2010 until 2017.

Throughout these serious allegations Assange maintained his innocence; however, these troublesome charges served as a satisfactory red herring. They implied that Assange's persona was one of a selfish and morally ambiguous nature, a man that couldn't be trusted with his peers—much less national secrets.

These considerations lent legitimacy to the state official/international reaction that WikiLeaks was a dangerous organization. Even after Sweden dropped its allegations in 2017, the debate of WikiLeaks and Julian Assange still has a overtone of character assessment rather than analysis of WikiLeaks revelations.

Red herring tactics work as a facet of limited hangouts, by way of introducing new information for the purposes of creating social static. An integral component in addressing social issues and reforming practices is transparency of the related subject matter, a task that becomes more difficult as the nature of discussion becomes vague. By releasing or manufacturing information that appears to be sordid or otherwise specialized, the public demand for full transparency is satiated in lieu of a sensationalized narrative.

Furthermore it can be mentioned that, as with systems of government, there is no true binary to the rhetoric behind operations of state. While the leaking of information can lead to a push for more responsible state conduct, it can also lead to a compromising of individual safety. What remains unclear with many limited hangout and red herring constructs is the extent to which they exist for public safety or a means to perpetuate entrenched power.

The limited hangout serves as a means to placate the need for democratic process. In the three-fold paradox this is a non-negotiable requirement. If democracy of information and debate appear stifled, governments stand to lose credibility, both domestically and in the international hierarchy. While these misconstrued debates undermine true democratic process, they fulfill a public expectation that political progressivism will continue to evolve.

Stay-Behind

Closely related to the practice of proxy warfare is the use of *stay-behind operations*. These clandestine functions exist as a means of inflammatory covert warfare and as insurance against enemy expansionism. Stay-behind missions consist of paramilitary cells that are left in domestic, neutral, or enemy territory. For domestic purposes these "secret armies" exist as a hidden means to ward off enemy invasion.

During World War II the United Kingdom initiated secretive auxiliary units in preparation for a potential invasion by the Nazis, recruiting and training paramilitary troops for domestic guerrilla warfare. In Nazi Germany this was mirrored by Werwolf, a stay-behind militia that aimed to counter Allied advancement if they were to enter Nazi territory.

Also known as *clandestine cell systems* or *sleeper cells* covert armies are far from uncommon. Such fail-safes have existed in dozens of countries including Portugal, Finland, Turkey, and more. The defensive benefit is obvious, as is the surrounding secrecy. Were these armies to be well known to the public their defensive efficacy would be limited.

Similar considerations apply for neutral nations. In order to prevent the expansion of rival countries, large world powers may institute veiled armies in regionally associated nations. The most popular reference to these practices would be the stay-behind coalitions created by NATO, made to prevent advancement of the Soviet Union during the Cold War.

Secret armies under the codename Operation Gladio were created throughout the landmass of Europe to deter potential Soviet expansionism, procured by Western powers and the North Atlantic Treaty Organization. However, in neutral nations these contingency plans come at a peculiar and concerning cost.

A general issue with the demographic of stay-behind operatives is the zeal needed to procure such professionals. To counter the Soviet Union, there had to be a prevailing opposition to the ideology of communism in NATO's Gladio armies. This would ultimately attract individuals with intense nationalist beliefs, often bordering on the xenophobic convictions held by former fascist nations such as Germany and Italy. The extremism fostered by these operations was not only permitted, but to an extent encouraged, as a means to keep the USSR at bay without formal forces from the United States.

While there is some skepticism around the involvement of Gladio operatives, leftist Italian moments between the 1960s and 1980s were fraught with opposition violence. Amounting to approximately two thousand deaths in the form of bombings, street warfare, and assassinations, political tensions were raised significantly under the dual shadow of both the Soviets and NATO.

Even though no state confirmed evidence has been shown connecting Gladio to these attacks, Italy's left-wing resurgence was the exact political movement NATO's stay-behind army was meant to counter. No doubt there was potential for nationalist right-wing terrorism in the use of Gladio, just as there would be for left-wing terrorism in a USSR based stay-behind operation. In essence the mentality behind such armies requires a distilled mindset of its handler. Without extremist convictions, a stay-behind army in foreign territory would be ineffective in the face of sudden adversity.

Another instance of political zeal being used in clandestine cells existed in the militant groups that became the Viet Cong.

After the Geneva Accord separated Vietnam into Northern and Southern provinces, militias such as the National Liberation Front banded together in order to form a united presence opposing former Vietnamese Emperor Bao Dai. While North Vietnam embraced communism as a result of backlash against their former monarchy, the South began journeying toward a decentralized pseudo-capitalist government. Oddly enough, this new Southern government still retained Vietnam's former emperor as its figurehead.

This decision merited a predictable response from many Vietnamese citizens, helping to foster political unrest throughout the south in the form of the Viet Cong. While Western nations portrayed these combatants as a facet of Hanoi's communist regime in the north, many were actually southern citizens who had extreme distaste for the former emperor to remain in power. In a situation reminiscent of the Iranian shah, dissent and revolutionary political action were implied in such a scenario.

Funding trickled down from the Soviet Union to Hanoi, and eventually found its way to the southern Viet Cong. The VC were able to use such capital to wage guerrilla warfare in the south. There was widespread dissatisfaction with the newly implemented power structure in Southern Vietnam, so finding new VC recruits would not prove difficult.

The situation was further stressed in 1963 as a power struggle between former emperor Dai and his selected president Ngo Diem came to a head. Diem was overthrown in a coup, showing intense weakness to nations such as Russia and China that sought to take Saigon and Vietnam's South.

The internal dispute in Saigon led to heightened guerrilla activity from Vietnamese clandestine cells, and eventually amounted to full-on US involvement following the Gulf of Tonkin incident. Interestingly enough, this justification for war on the part of the United States is also veiled in some uncertainty.

On August 4, 1964, the USS Maddox and USS Turner were receiving sonar signals that seemed to imply an attack from North Vietnam. They destroyed what they had thought were Vietnamese submarines, yet no wreckage or bodies were found. Assuming that the attack had been legitimate, President Johnson opted for retaliatory attacks on nearby submarine outposts.

Though he assured the Soviets that no further American involvement would occur following the strikes, it would only be a few short days before Congress passed the Southeast Asia Resolution. This granted Johnson license to initiate full warfare in communist Asian nations without legislative oversight.

Commenting on the Gulf incident privately in 1965 President Johnson is quoted: "For all I know, our navy was shooting at whales out there."

The escalation of Vietnam's long war, US involvement, and the painful road to unification was undoubtedly fueled by the use of stay-behind operations.

These operations are often meant to create inflammatory responses and provocations for full-scale warfare. The zealotry of stay-behind militants is paramount to the success of the operation. Fast and deadly response is needed, as is emotional investment in the cause. While some guerrilla operatives may be profit motivated, it is far more reliable to rest laurels on the shoulders of a political or moral conviction.

False Flag

Quite possibly one of the most controversial of hidden state operations is the *false flag*. Shrouded by endless debate, conspiracy, and skepticism, there is a considerable degree of disbelief regarding the use of such tactics; as such the primary focus of this section will be upon confirmed events rather than the realm of the hypothetical.

A false flag exists for the purpose of directly initiating political reform, occupation of territory, or heightening domestic security for the purposes of power consolidation. In order to perform these actions it once again becomes imperative to command civilian consent, using the extreme measures of false flagging.

In these scenarios a government, international coalition, or intelligence agency will perform either a fake or real attack on friendly territory, blaming the attack on a foreign entity that will yield the desired spoils of war or security.

Elaborating, if Nation A wishes to commandeer the resources of Nation B it could use a false flag. By performing a fake attack on its own soil Nation A could place the blame for said attack on its target. This effectively creates license for the use of military force against Nation B. It seems morally detestable, as it may also seem far-fetched, yet such strategies exist well beyond just speculation.

One of the most famous false flagging accounts is known as the Gleiwitz incident. After the fall of Nazi Germany a series of international hearings were conducted for the purposes of sentencing war criminals, known as the Nuremberg Trials. It was in these trials that SS official Alfred Naujocks testified to the use of a covert operation in German Upper Silesia, for the purposes of warranting an invasion of Poland.

On August 31st 1939 a group of German operatives was placed under order of SS commanders Reinhard Heydrich and Heinrich Muller to stage an attack on a rural radio outpost located in Gleiwitz. The operatives were to dress as Polish soldiers and broadcast anti-German propaganda from the site. In tandem to this, prisoners from the concentration camp of Dachau were executed and posed to look like Polish saboteurs on location. Their faces were disfigured, and other means of identification were altered to provide "evidence" of a Polish advance into Germany.

The events at Gleiwitz were a small part of a larger propaganda offensive dubbed Operation Himmler—where German railways, forest service stations, communications relays, and individuals were targeted by falsified Polish militias. This was on the heels of recent claims by Hitler's government that Polish authorities had been campaigning for the ethnic cleansing of Germans in Poland, as well as the potential for a Polish front to enter German territories.

On September 1 Fall Weiss was initiated, an invasion of Poland by Germany that began the Second World War. Hitler cited the Himmler attacks during his speech at the Reichstag as justification for invasion, using falsified evidence to support the agenda.

Another event of significance occurred in Manchuria, China, 1931. Tensions had been high between the Japanese and Chinese governments after the Russo-Japanese War in the early 1900s. Even though the war resolution had granted the Japanese use of China's South Manchurian Railways, there was dissonance pertaining to rights and privileges associated with said use. Specifically, the Japanese government was dissatisfied with its rights in the region compared to the greater trade-related autonomy that Russia seemed to enjoy from its neighbors in China.

Economic longevity on the Asian mainland was of extreme consequence for Japan; its trade assets in China required expansion and permanence.

Without means of diplomatic resolve to these concerns, it was in 1931 that lieutenant Suemori Kawamoto put into action a plan to detonate a small amount of dynamite at the Japanese Railway in Manchuria, placing blame for said event on Chinese dissidents. What was to follow would be a full-scale offensive from the Japanese Empire that resulted in the occupation of Manchuria and creation of the temporary Japanese puppet state of Manchukuo. A League of Nations investigation known as the Lytton Report later determined the true origin of the railway explosion, expelling Japan in 1933.

In the 1950s another false flagging occurred, this time at the command of the Israeli government under minister Pinhas Lavon.

Circa 1922, Egypt had been gradually shedding the occupation of British forces and establishing a stronger national identity in the Middle East. A paramount concern with this was the trade use of the ever-valuable Suez Canal in Sinai, and the distaste many Arab nations had for Israel. The Straits of Tiran were off limits already to Israeli trade. This made Lavon's government desperate to keep British presence in the Sinai, and an effective way to do so would be demonstrating domestic instability in Egypt.

A covert engagement known as Operation Susannah was put into action in 1954, wherein Egyptian guerrillas were hired by the Israeli military to plant bombs in sensitive locations. These locations would include Egyptian, British, and American civilian targets—such as cinemas, education centers, and libraries. The damages from the explosions would then be attributed to factions of the Muslim Brotherhood, communists, and nationalists as a means to promote further British occupation of Egypt; thereby ensuring continued access to the Suez by Israel.

Two operatives of Operation Susannah were tried and convicted by Egypt, forcing Minister Lavon to resign.

Other than the goals of occupation and warfare, false flagging also has a primary objective of consolidating power or ethnic margins via use of xenophobic security measures. For instance, in the 1980s three terrorist bombings were conducted in France, targeting the cities of Paris, Cannes, and Nice. These attacks were meant to incite tensions between French Muslims and Jews, ultimately to the agenda of French and European nationalism. Posing as a Zionist group, the perpetrators of the bombings chose civilian and religious targets. They left anti-Muslim propaganda and Jewish symbols such as the Star of David at the scenes of destruction.

Ideally to the guilty parties, this would have succeeded in not only heightening tensions between the Muslims and Jews—but also would've warranted a greater measure of security from the French government against migrants and people of Middle Eastern descent. The end goal of these attacks was to create a more demographically homogeneous European nation.

In a similar fashion to stay-behind operations, false flag events often hinge on ideological, political, and religious zeal or profit motivation. On the right-wing spectrum this often coincides with nationalism, or aims to homogenize national diversity. On the left-wing spectrum this may shift to aims of removing entrenched power and redistribution of authority or liquidity to the masses.

To a greater degree of relevance, however, each use of false flagging (regardless of political orientation) serves to mislead the public into subversive agendas, by way of manipulating the opinion of the masses against a foreign entity.

A final review of false flag operations comes in the form of a proposal by the US Joint Chiefs of Staff circa 1962. Cuban independence had been a thorn in the side of Western nations for some time, from perspectives of both trade use and military strategy. Cuba's alliance with the Soviet Union was also a considerable subject of concern for the United States.

The US Joint Chiefs of Staff and Department of Defense were prepared to take drastic action. Approved by chairman Lyman Lemnitzer, a plan was made to provide pretext for an American invasion of Cuba by means of false flagging American institutions, civilians, and infrastructure.

Suggested ways to do this were hijacking aircrafts, sinking boats in American or Cuban territories, blowing up military property, and orchestrating attacks on American civilians. Each of these options could either be performed by actual Cuban terrorists under US hire, or fabricated by US government operatives. If manufactured correctly this could create the outrage necessary from the public for the US to go to war with Cuba.

Operations Northwoods, Mongoose, and Bingo had treasonous implications—yet each was green-lighted by their respective agencies. The Kennedy Administration blocked said plans, each of them only becoming public in 1997 via the Freedom of Information Act.

The Soviets under Khrushchev and Stalin, Britain's MI6, the CIA, Turkish Prime Minister Bayar, NATO, Mossad, the SADF, as well as factions all the way from Columbia to Algeria have been privy to suggested (or functional) false flag attacks. The veiled nature of these creations makes it very hard to discern reality from fiction; in fact, that is their very purpose.

It becomes imperative to use critical thought, as well as an analysis of any potential beneficiaries to events in question.

Schismatic Operations

While the limited hangout, stay-behind, and false flag exist (in some capacity) to unify public support or discussion, it often becomes necessary for entrenched power to create divide amongst the citizenry as well. The purpose for this is to deflect criticism and controversy away from established institutions, and realign said social tension to exist between conflicting domestic groups.

In other words, to achieve a desired foreign goal, unity must be manufactured amongst the people; while to maintain entrenched power domestically, social divide becomes the primary objective. Such a tried and true method of divide and conquer has been utilized throughout history, yet its existence in the United States provides a perfect case study.

Beginning in 1676, the British ruling elite had a significant problem in their American colonies. There had recently been a harsh and violent rebellion in Jamestown, Virginia, wherein African slaves and European indentured servants had staged a coup against colonial governor Sir William Berkeley. The reasons for the rebellion were primarily attributed to policies related to westward expansion and interaction with Native Americans, but also had much to do with modification of rights to the servant classes.

African slaves and European servants found they had much in common insofar as treatment-related grievances, and in their interactions with each other were able to unify under common goals to initiate a formal uprising.

Bacon's Rebellion holds an interesting historical perspective on race and hierarchy in the United States. What is significant in particular is the unity between both the white and black underclass, poised against a draconian system of entrenched British power. The mingling of slave and servant laborers allowed rights-related injustices to build upon a foundation of personal liberties rather than racial margins, creating a formidable insurrection. News of the rebellion was met with very reasonable concern in the United Kingdom. Jamestown had been burned to the ground and Berkeley's militia retreated, forcing the hand of the British Navy to quell the revolutionaries.

Following these events it became obvious to the British colonial elite that racial lines had to be hardened between servants and slaves, so as to prevent another unification of force from the underclass. The fraternizing between these groups had enabled a revolt that had shaken the very foundation of Virginia's colony, and had to be addressed if the British power structure wished to remain intact.

Henceforth, racial divide would be implemented and condoned, creating a separation between slaves and indentured servants. Aside from the direct social meaning of this, a further analysis meant the creation of rhetorical divide as well; an encouragement of racist ideology and cultivation of its acceptance in the future United States.

Time progressed and Bacon's Rebellion faded into distant memory while the fledgling US fought for its independence. Yet even amongst the famous backdrop of "all men are created equal," there was a grueling disparity in such altruistic words. Slavery of the Africans and westward expansion into Native American lands were both staunch realities, as were gender-based and religious subjugations. Power was no longer held by the British over the colonies, and a new issue became apparent to America's designers.

The rest of the world (certainly the larger powers) had a strong foothold in global economics, military strength, and international relationships. Even other colonies in the New World were under stewardship of nations like France and Spain, leaving the United States in a precarious position. This new nation could afford very little time to establish itself in the global spectrum, or risk being overtaken by foreign powers that no doubt would seek to use the vast wealth of North America for their own expansion.

Three things became extremely apparent:

1. The need for continued slave labor as a means to ensure economic output in the extreme. Many other colonial nations had utilized such tactics and greatly heightened their position in the international hierarchy, making it clear to the architects of the United States that such a heinous practice would ultimately manifest a strong, relevant nation.

2. The inevitability of the eventual and gradual breaking of native treaties, as well as Westward expansion. While Native Americans were promised their own sovereign nations by the European settlers, they possessed a lack of military fortitude in comparison to foreign nations that would ultimately put American borders at risk for invasion. This, of course, was a secondary point to a likely desire of simply usurping land and resources from the indigenous peoples of North America.

3. The necessity that the revolutionary power of the colonies not revolt and overthrow the new US government. Should the revolution give way to another revolution it would show exploitable weakness in the USA, an alluring invitation for foreign invasion or meddling. To deter this reality there would need to be a monopoly of power to only

men of a certain age, and monopoly of education to margins of only a certain class.

Even though this nation would be unified in the rhetoric of equality, it could not truly be equal. For the United States to pack thousands of years of development into two centuries it would require slavery, expansionism, and internal divide amongst the citizens.

Progressing well into the 1800s these schismatic maneuvers were only interrupted by the Civil War, wherein the Northern and Southern states clashed over economic stakes. Tones of racial equality and freedom of the slaves were utilized for the purposes of using moral debt to rally support for the war effort. Even after the Emancipation and Reconstruction, ex-slaves were subject to repressive legislative codes, intense judicial protocol, and an overall maintained degree of separation from whites. The North, for all its moral luster, did relatively little to curb this post-war dystopia.

Acting on the staple of westward expansion and alienation of the natives, Lincoln's government held powerful distaste for the American Indian. While advertising equality and justice on behalf of the slaves, there were attacks and slaughters of the Sioux, Navajo, and Cherokee. These included the intentional defaulting on government payments to the natives, the burning of crops, removal of resources from native lands, and the execution of countless individuals.

Entering the twentieth century, blacks, women, and natives were still not allowed to vote. Jim Crow laws continued to separate the black underclass from the white underclass in the continued spirit of the aftermath following Bacon's Rebellion. Even post-Jim Crow and the initiation of civil rights, women's suffrage, and updated native rights in the 1950s, there would be new barriers erected to marginalize the American population.

Conveniently it would only be a few short years after these progressive strides that the War on Drugs would take effect under President Nixon. The penalties for drug use and possession would yield results that would antagonize the lower-middle class while turning a blind eye to aristocratic use or commerce. Namely these federal ultimatums would be destined to target a disproportionate number of blacks and Hispanics in urban regions, while levying the same biased charges against lower-class whites in rural areas. These configurations are phrased elegantly by Michelle Alexander in her book *The New Jim Crow* (2010):

> *The genius of the current caste system, and what most distinguishes it from its predecessors, is that it appears voluntary. People choose to commit crimes, and that's why they are locked up or locked out, we are told. This feature makes the politics of responsibility particularly tempting, as it appears the system can be avoided with good behavior. But herein lies the trap. All people make mistakes. All of us are sinners. All of us are criminals. All of us violate the law at some point in our lives. In fact, if the worst thing you have ever done is speed ten miles over the speed limit on the freeway, you have put yourself and others at more risk of harm than someone smoking marijuana in the privacy of his or her living room. Yet there are people in the United States serving life sentences for first-time drug offenses, something virtually unheard of anywhere else in the world.*

Another reads:

> *In the era of colorblindness, it is no longer socially permissible to use race, explicitly, as a justification for discrimination, exclusion, and social contempt. So we*

don't. Rather than rely on race, we use our criminal justice system to label people of color "criminals" and then engage in all the practices we supposedly left behind. Today it is perfectly legal to discriminate against criminals in nearly all the ways that it was once legal to discriminate against African-Americans. Once you're labeled a felon, the old forms of discrimination—employment discrimination, housing discrimination, denial of the right to vote, denial of educational opportunity, denial of food stamps and other public benefits, and exclusion from jury service—are suddenly legal. As a criminal, you have scarcely more rights, and arguably less respect, than a black man living in Alabama at the height of Jim Crow. We have not ended racial caste in America; we have merely redesigned it.

Illustrating the initial purpose of Bacon's Rebellion is truly invaluable while finding use for these methods in modern applications. Obviously power structures have shifted, morphed, and changed altogether since 1676. The successful repression of this massive number of people has served as a model for each incoming power system, allowing power to transfer without interference from said masses.

Schismatic operations aren't always so overt. Many take the form of polarized media outlets' efforts to devalue and delegitimize public opinion or create strife based on social freedoms.

In essence, these largely domestic programs serve as a smokescreen to conceal entrenched power, allowing established-determinism to continue unabated. As with the outcome of Bacon's Rebellion, there is much to do with social schisms that rely on the complicity and reaction of the populace. Historical narratives, racial or ethnic barriers, and expectations of government can all be easily altered.

Notes

A focal point of this section has been confirmed evidence for *operations of state.* As a necessity to the content, speculation has been avoided in the above-stated events so as to provide reasonable context for each subject. Sadly, this limits the historical vantage point for many of these functions.

Operations of state are meant to be covert by their nature. Many throughout history may have gone unnoticed or unconfirmed. Referencing these would serve little purpose for the sake of illustrating legitimacy, yet many unconfirmed examples have truly captivating backgrounds and compelling evidence.

It is through critical thought that we can identify and consider applications for these operations. As the process of globalization alters and removes entrenched power, manifestations of these hidden agendas will become even more important to identify. When major global powers shift we must be able to identify who and what they are.

Globalization

No two countries that both had McDonald's had fought a war against each other since each got its McDonald's.
—Thomas Friedman

Neoliberalization has not been very effective in revitalizing global capital accumulation, but it has succeeded remarkably well in restoring, or in some instances (as in Russia and China) creating, the power of an economic elite. The theoretical utopianism of neoliberal argument has, I conclude, primarily worked as a system of justification and legitimation for whatever needed to be done to achieve this goal.
—David Harvey

There are two globalizations . . . The elite globalization represents minority forces. The elite globalization is about making money . . . The people's globalization, the democratic mass globalization is about life values.
—Kevin Danaher

I find that because of modern technological evolution and our global economy, and as a result of the great increase in population, our world has greatly changed: it has become much smaller. However, our perceptions have not evolved at the same pace; we continue to cling to old national demarcations and the old feelings of "us" and "them."
—Dalai Lama

The lack of monetary discipline has become a hallmark of unfettered globalization. Central banks have failed to provide a stable underpinning to world financial

markets and to an increasingly asset-dependent global economy.
—Stephen Roach, former chairman for Asia and chief economist for Morgan Stanley

The trends that are shaping the twenty-first century world embody both promise and peril. Globalization, for example, has lifted hundreds of millions of people out of poverty while contributing to social fragmentation and a massive increase in inequality, not to mention serious environmental damage.
—Klaus Schwab

Keynesianism, if you add its flexible, muscular form during the Depression to its more rigid postwar version, lasted forty-five years. Our own globalization, with its technocratic and technological determinism and market idolatry, had thirty years. And now it too is dead.
—John Ralston Saul

With the development of industrial capitalism, a new and unanticipated system of injustice, it is libertarian socialism that has preserved and extended the radical humanist message of the Enlightenment and the classical liberal ideals that were perverted into an ideology to sustain the emerging social order.
—Noam Chomsky

Many historians and economists have noted that globalization has come in waves. The modern globalized world stands on the shoulders of its predecessors, making an increasingly unified landscape for world governments, industries, and citizens. It becomes no exaggeration to describe the earth as "flat" in terms of its connectivity.

When financial markets crash in the United States, waves are felt all the way from Seoul to London. When oil embargos or deficits occur in the Middle East, emergency contingencies are enacted from Germany to Los Angeles. The idea of this "flat" earth acknowledges a reality that supersedes past globalized worlds, a true connection of successes and failures that the entire world must share. With economic markets intertwined and the rising expectations of global democracy and individualism, as well as the efforts to decentralize power structures, there is an ironic undertone of socialism to such a massive capitalist construct.

Whether this "succeed or fail" ultimatum extends to the economic elite is another subject altogether. Regarding the fate of nations as well as the world's citizenry, there is a heightened connectivity between all regions of the world.

Globalization largely occurred in the past for colonial reasons. The assimilation of peoples and resources were acceptable from the perspective of conquest. While this mindset still exists today it is veiled. There is an expectation for societies (global and otherwise) to increase the quality of life for people all over the world. This means that democracy is expected to spread, individual liberties should expand, and elite accountability should be more comprehensive.

The current incarnation of globalization serves to both help and hinder these notions. Though the spread of heightened life quality surely exists in many measures, sheer demand for more products means harsh labor environments for some. Democracy (as illustrated) can be easily faked by imposter governments, or derailed through many means. Accountability for the aristocratic elite is far more feasible now than ever before in the past, yet so is the potential for widespread corruption. With each gain there is also potential loss.

A truly "flat" earth would convey a playing field without peaks or valleys. Should the plain flood, everyone would deal with the rising water. Should it yield a bountiful harvest, everyone would share the spoils. While this new world is surely flatter than its predecessors, it is far from being a level playing field. Indeed, while the plains are expanding quickly, there are still towering mountains, deep chasms, and thick forests.

Democracy of Information

In 2007 a British newspaper called *The Observer* published an exposé on Gap clothing and its ties to child labor in Delhi, India. *Newspaper*, being a somewhat outdated term at this point, meant that such sensitive information about Gap clothing had been released to the currents of the internet. Tremendous momentum would follow as people across the world reacted in outrage. This could have yielded a lowered profit margin for Gap, perhaps even a permanent loss in client base. Confronted with the issue en masse, Gap was forced to make a public statement and plan to eliminate child labor from their production, as well as give hefty sums of money to the affected children's families.

This is likely one of thousands (if not millions) of instances where the internet has been used as a tool to create ethical standards for industry. When consumers saw the implications of their purchases from Gap they had to make one of two choices: either ignore the moral issues regarding child labor or stop creating demand for it. Without the internet as a medium to convey the story worldwide it may have only been readers of *The Observer* that knew of such practices; certainly not enough people to take on a multinational company and force them to change.

Reimagining this, the internet serves as both a window and a mirror. Through such a unified medium one has the option to see the impact of their choices in consumption, the standards of the industries they support, and the political ideologies of said industries. The internet provides a new kind of democracy in which the public forum is augmented to an unprecedented extreme. These democratic ideals take the shape of the informed consumer, the unaligned partisan, and the pioneers of market creativity.

In earlier times perhaps a library would contain a zeitgeist of human knowledge for reference. Yet as the rows and shelves of books came to an end, so did the knowledge they contained. Gaps in these subjects could range from entire cultures to entire centuries, troubling narrative monopolies, or bans on certain information. All of these barriers are shattered by the megalith of internet expansion. Suddenly all subjects have coverage regardless of origin or timeline. Multiple narratives can be sourced and cross-referenced, bans on information (even classified documents) are effectively useless.

An obvious subject in this vein would be government information that is made public through outlets like WikiLeaks, whose release of classified material provides an opportunity for democratic discussion to formerly classified events. Regardless of the implications or morality relating to the release of said information, there is little argument that it allows for the public to be included in formerly closed subject matter. Even on a more basic level the democracy of information has a profound impact on average people worldwide, and will only increase exponentially as more people gain access to the internet.

Gaining insight into the practices of consumer companies is only the beginning. For instance, one can easily reference political, ethnic, geographical, and personal histories for nearly everything, providing context for the world that currently exists. Hopefully it has been conveyed thus far in this book that context is truly everything. The past determines what the future will hold.

In 1967 the Freedom of Information Act (FOIA) went into effect under President Lyndon B. Johnson. The FOIA allowed for previously classified government information to be released to the public based upon request and purpose. Such releases have included FBI threats to Martin Luther King Jr., government surveillance initiatives/plans, SEC documentations, testing of biological agents in the US, and much more. This legislation incurred a massive amount of potential clarity into government functions, only further augmented by the free flow of information on the internet. Having the ability to see into former policy helped to create curiosity that would evolve into the current public forum of internet use, likely inspiring many of the leak sources that now provoke intense discussion about the roles and morality of government.

It comes as no surprise that because of non-state-sanctioned outlets like WikiLeaks, the Obama administration began denying approximately 75 percent of FOIA requests. As limited informational outlets like the FOIA gave way to true democratic forums like WikiLeaks the FOIA began to erode in its accessibility. Referencing the societal foundation of security, access to secure information has to be monopolized (to a degree) for systemic power to remain intact. The removal of checks and balances from the classification of information puts entrenched power into jeopardy. The timing of these two events is far from coincidental; as the rise of leak sources and alt-media began, so did the removal of FOIA leniency.

Also consider that FOIA requests increased dramatically in volume during this time. No doubt this came as a result of increasing public involvement, curiosity, and concern with state affairs that were likely linked to heightened availability of information.

Let's frame these events in contrast to many ancient civilizations.

In Egypt during the time of the Pharaohs literacy and writing were privileges that were controlled by religious, state, and military elite. The same can be said for many old societies, the Dark Ages in Europe being another prime example. By only permitting written record to be accessed or created by select tiers of a society, said tiers could easily fabricate or homogenize narratives, retain selective traditions, and perpetuate power structures.

Individual accounts of specific events could not be recorded by those who were illiterate. Therefore, historical details and counter-narratives were likely lost in these societies. Oral tradition would lose its detail as well, while written tradition could easily be recounted. Above all else the great zeitgeists of these societies were only accessible to a select few, leaving the majority of the population to act as simple laborers. Many ancient people existed to perpetuate an economy and mantle that they would never truly have access to.

Now to modernize this concept:

The widespread promotion of literacy, the printing press, the radio, and eventually the invention of the television news network bolstered informational connectivity in the world. People could now understand their political climate and global events, also learning about the world around them. As a result many superstitions would begin to fade, cultural biases could begin to dissolve, and educational foundation for the masses would be ultimately elevated. While pockets of the world still lacked these amenities, these developments created unprecedented rises in per capita educational standards. Even beyond basic schooling there was now potential for many to learn in a more broad and comprehensive way. Yet even these inventions were hardly enough to truly democratize information.

In order to own a printing press, broadcast on wide-ranging radio bands, or obtain access to transmit news on television, there were prerequisites. Capital would be the defining factor as to how accessible these outlets would be, and capital would be consolidated to an economic elite that often worked hand in hand with state or private aristocracies. Margins for narratives, traditions, and hierarchy would still exist. So long as formidable capital was required to participate in these modernized public forums there couldn't be true democratic involvement in informational conduits. For informational democracy to work capital would have to be irrelevant regarding the ability to voice opinions or gather accurate information.

This is precisely why the internet has completely decimated its predecessors in terms of raising equality and accessibility. While fees are still applied to have an internet connection, public places also offer entrance to the vast world of electronic information at each one of our fingertips. Schools, coffee shops, and public places offer connectivity to a medium that allows everyone to not only contribute in global discussion but also to learn from each other. To another equally intense degree, the spectrum of economics has also become "flat." Monetary exchange and liquidity have never been easier to navigate, consumer products are easily obtained, and the great markets of the world can be easily accessed by anyone with internet connection.

Compared to the exclusivity harkened in humanity's collective past, this is monumental. What is even more monumental is the speed at which this connectivity has changed from the printing press to an intertwined network extending beyond social class, language, nationality, and ethnicity.

The "flat" earth now regards information as the greatest commodity, the most powerful weapon, the ultimate fuel. The Pandora's box of literacy and the public forum holds the key to decentralization of power, likely even the promise of libertarian or anarchic ideals that have barely been touched upon in the past. If narratives can be challenged history is no longer written by the victor. If traditions can be diversified status quo can be altered and secularity promoted. If hierarchy can be recycled despotism can be avoided.

Each of these factors harken themselves to a previously made point—namely that for involved and progressive societies to exist there must be heightened participation from the citizenry. The dual face of this is the concerns of the great philosophers, that average individuals have no context for making large-scale public decisions. As time proceeds these concerns become more and more speculative. The amount of informed involvement with social affairs now rests with the effort of the individual, to provide context for themselves through the medium of internet use.

This is not to say that the anonymity or vague setting of the internet is not without potential for corruption. Quite the contrary. In 2016 Wells Fargo Bank had to fire over five thousand employees who had been operating fake accounts for the purposes of extortion through phony bank dues and fees. These accounts were made official largely through fabrication of email addresses and online profiles, making false individuals just real enough to be profited off of. This came, of course, at the expense of actual account holders, given that fees and dues were deducted from company accounts whose capital pool consisted of Wells Fargo customer funds.

Given the degree of ease with which one can manufacture an identity online, the potential for corrupt usage becomes clear. This also applies to instances of personal information being put on the dark web for purchase.

As a whole it would seem that the increased diversity of information, coupled with its level of availability, have already made accountability in global affairs a far more realistic prospect. While much of the developing world remains offline, there still exists a massive influx of voices from all around the globe, all of which actively change the reality of our flattening civilization. Should the budding world of internet connectivity be extended en masse to sub-Saharan Africa, Southeast Asia, Central America, and the Middle East, one can only imagine the wealth of interaction and revolutionary social or economic ideas that could be cultivated.

It would seem that the next great peak of human sociology is currently being created via unification under a digital public forum. Former plateaus that existed were constrained by traditional power-related dogmas, that one by one seem to lose pertinence in the face of this new "flat" earth. This mutation of civilization also comes at a heavy cost. When tradition is lost or changed many world cultures become diluted, to eventually remain no more.

Cultural Homogenization

On the Greek island of Evia unusual sounds can be heard, drifting lightly through the nearby valleys. Upon first listen it is reminiscent of bird calls, detailed whistles that pierce long distances and nearby winds from the Aegean Sea. However, the origin of these tones is not birds at all. They come from the villagers of Antia where the townspeople have used whistling as a language for centuries.

While this isn't the only instance of a whistle-language, it is critically endangered—being the least used language in Europe. It is called Sfyria and has been passed down from generation to generation, only to finally yield in the shadow of the "flat" earth.

Prior to the twentieth century it is likely that this Grecian subset was as successful as any other village, yet as modernization was put into high gear the number of Sfyria speakers began to dwindle. A few decades ago there would only be 250 speakers. Then only an approximate 30. Now a humble 6 people are the last remaining Sfyria speakers. Why do the concepts of globalization and culture have mutually exclusive qualities?

For Sfyria, globalization meant the younger generations would continue to move away from Antia in pursuit of bigger economic dreams. The simple shepherding life of their ancestors did not hold the same allure as it may have had in the past. Thus, the language is not passed on as it had been. Even if it were taught to younger Antians they likely would not use Sfyria in societies outside of Antia, letting the language slowly perish.

Of course the people of Antia are but one example of diversity that is becoming rarer. It is not limited to small cultural margins; even large-scale religious and regional demographics now find themselves at the mercy of a more uniformed planet. The concern of the whistling people of Greece is shared by Buddhists in Tibet and India. Decades of antagonization from the neighboring Chinese government had already made retaining Buddhism in this part of the world an uphill endeavor. As the world globalized it became clear to many of these Buddhists that they had other options outside of the monasteries.

Ancient Buddhist traditions and communities have become splintered due to a loss of numbers to the outside world, where for all its political correctness a certain cultural ambiguity serves the marketplace far better than specific traditions. Even for those who stay in their communities and continue the work of their ancestors, winds of change rock old customs.

For many farmers across the globe the rise in genetically modified food production has the potential to upset their way of life. It is not the higher yield of crops nor the elemental resistance that has a negative effect on the farmers of the world, but rather the ever-morphing legality and logistics that surround GMO harvesting. This is made very apparent in India, where an approximate two hundred thousand farmers have ended their own lives since 1995.

This massive tragedy is linked congruently with increased debt and destructive economics, each an operative of globalization and neoliberal trade. Several factors contribute to the sadness plaguing India's farms.

In the late '90s the World Trade Organization allied with corporate monoliths Monsanto, Cargill, and Syngenta to pressure the World Bank for monopoly of its seed stores. The World Bank had traditionally been responsible for (among much else) maintaining a literal library of seeds from all over the world, cataloging a staggering amount of biodiversity. Every strain, of each crop, from every part of the world had its own strengths and weaknesses. Many India-specific seeds would obviously do well in India, and should Indian farmers ever have a seed shortage, the World Bank could step in to help avoid a crisis.

As state capitalist companies moved to replace traditional seed stores they did so with products that were not only flawed, but antagonizing to the farming community.

One major issue would be that many proprietary corporate seeds are not designed for renewal. They do not pass on renewable traits to new generations of crops. Each season farmers must buy more seeds from Big Farma. Seeds had previously been a free resource that came with the knowledge of farming tradition, in many cases dating back hundreds or thousands of years. Most proprietary seeds need specific fertilizers and pesticides to grow at all, which as one may guess are also sold by Big Farma.

By implementing blanket sales of their products, major companies like Monsanto also play a dangerous and tragic game with the balance of ecology. Many batches of seeds given to India's farmers are not ideal for the environment in India. Farmers are forced under monopoly to purchase specific non-renewable seeds that are unable to grow well in India's climate. This means massive amounts of bankruptcy, poverty, and eventual suicides. Countless years of crop breeding and survival tradition in India would ultimately be cast aside in favor of profit-based motives.

Undermining such biodiversity gives rise to monocultures, a genetic uniformity of crops and resources. Much like human beings, or any other living creature, a stable population in plants requires genetic diversity. This applies not only to breeding and harvesting, but also to accommodating the vastly different environments on planet Earth.

This is not to say that GMO research and products have no intrinsic value. In many cases these creations can have much benefit for developing nations, provided that a monopoly of food and development aren't allowed to undermine said potential.

Aside from ecological and breeding specifics there is also a legal level to the globalized GMO monopoly. In this new "flat" earth lines blur between what is public and what is private. While Tesla opts to meet this new paradigm with a will to raise economic and societal standards, many Big Farma conglomerates often do not extend the same generosity.

Seed dispersal occurs naturally in a variety of ways. Be they blown by wind, carried by water, or moved by animals, all seeds must be moved to propagate new varieties of species. In the case of GMO products that are capable of seed renewal this sets in motion a whole new variety of problems.

Let's say two farmers in Anytown, USA, were neighbors. One farmer opts to begin GMO cultivation, while his counterpart continues organic growth. Should seed dispersal occur from our GMO farmer's land to the organic farmer's land, the organic farmer may find himself in possession of GMO crops. The problem here would be that the organic farmer did not pay for his GMO product. Since these crops are copyrighted by Big Farma there is a potential for legal action, which is to the utter detriment of the non-GMO farmer. This natural transmission of seeds is used against independent farmers by the homogenized global industry.

In these ways it is neither beneficial for a crop to renew or not renew; extorting the buyer into perpetual purchases or facing independent farmers with imminent lawsuits. The homogeneity of the biosphere becomes clearly related to the homogeneity of the global "free market."

Suffice to say perhaps it isn't the forward-thinking ideas behind GMO use that are destructive as a whole, but rather their implementation. The crux of free market mass expansion is this:

The market design will initially promote better ideas by way of competitive business. The more competition in industry, the more functional products will rise to the top and dysfunctional models be removed. Think of it as economic Darwinism. However, let's say a company that sells intrinsic necessities (like food) manages to stake claim to the top tier of their industry. They will have an unfair advantage over the market and will become capable of suppressing competitors no matter how effective competitive models may be.

Profit-based output and free-market altruism have an ironic relationship.

While the globalized free market exists in theory to promote a higher standard of living for humankind, it is constrained by profit-motive. Paradoxically, globalized "free" market designs serve both as a means of improving on old models while suppressing competition. Effective ways to deal with market homogeneity on a global scale are scarce. The altruistic side of the "free" market's efficiency is viable for questioning.

This being said established-determinative markets (like those under 20th century communism) can possess the literal same issues of homogeneity and lack of upward mobility.

What is clear is that homogeneity of the market, while it should be a realistic concern, does not pervade every facet of industry. One amazing example of the expedited free market process is the airline industry.

In less than one hundred years human flight went from an isolated experiment by two brothers, on the Outer Banks of North Carolina, to a worldwide multi-billion-dollar industry. Not only this, but flight is also accessible to a staggering number of the world's population at reasonable cost and is a consistently safe way to travel.

Compare this to other inventions in history. Progress in industry expands exponentially based on the surrounding technology. For thousands of years written documents were the primary means of communication, yet in less than one hundred years humankind has graduated from the original telephone to literal handheld computers—capable of much more than just making calls.

Given these observations it may be easier to recognize industrial monopolies than previously noted. Given the great strides made in communication, medicine, science, and much more, it could be assumed that stagnant industries are likely monopolized. A prime candidate in this case would be automobiles and their respective petroleum-based fuel. Given that the internal-combustion engine has been in use since the 1800s, it comes as a surprise that this model is still the primary component for automobile use.

With the immense variety of other technologies that are diversifying and improving, it could be reasoned that petroleum companies and car companies have homogenized the global auto industry for nearly one hundred years.

While this hasn't prevented manufacturing of alternative vehicles in totality, it does beg the question of whether these petroleum alternatives could have been made available decades ago. For consumers it will be increasingly valuable to expect and demand progress from this industry as a means to prevent further monopoly.

These considerations, however, do not deal with the plight of the Mursi in Ethiopia, the Cocopah in the Southwest US, the Awa of the Amazon, or the Loba of the Himalayas. As globalized commerce becomes standardized so do cultural standards. No longer do the niched occupations of the world's peoples remain endemic to their respective locations; rather these formerly varied societies are being conformed to the standard of operation for the global economy. Perhaps one of the most obvious in traditional culture is the rapid decline of Christianity in the West.

According the Pew Research Center, a top source for demographic and figure analysis, individuals identifying as Christian have gone from 86 percent of Americans to 76 percent in a little over fifteen years. This couples with the influx of religiously-neutral millennials, whose generation has accompanied declines in most major US religions domestically. For instance, based on said survey analysis there are more religiously unaffiliated Americans than there are Catholic or Protestant Christians. Even within the margins of religion, hardline sectarianism is becoming rarer as secularism is embraced by more people.

The reason for the deterioration of institutional religion is correlated with the homogenization of endemic cultures. As diversity floods the world marketplace, goods and services become more universal in their availability. Economic niches are no longer confined to specific geographic areas, nor are endemic communal ties. Should one want a sushi dinner they no longer need to go to Japan. They can easily find a restaurant with such dishes in the US, England, or South

Africa. The same could be said for many goods and services that were formally specific to certain cultures.

The resulting mindset that this facilitates is one deeply rooted in individualism, self-determination, and opportunity. Generations that are born into this new "flat" world are exposed to the riches of the globe without the prerequisite of culture, though research into cultural origins is made easy by informational democracy.

In the larger scope this implies that the mentality of close-knit community becomes farther from reality; close-knit community being a companion of tradition and therefore indigenous culture. The global community grows in such a way that focus on small-scale community is increasingly lost, and with it the traditional or cultural variations that evolved with them.

The new generations that are born into such a world are shown and taught that they are masters of their own destinies, learning early that uniformity is not necessarily key to success. Rather than being told to find their place in a community and pass along deep-rooted tradition, modern generations are being told to pursue their dreams or passions. They are being told to think for themselves and find meaning that is personal to them, rather than carry the mantles of their ancestry.

This shift in priority will no doubt lead to the homogenization of many cultures, rendering the diversity of human beings to be ultimately lessened. While this wouldn't be the first time history has lost cultures and traditions, it may well be poised to be the most dramatic instance. But is this truly a bad thing?

The loss of tradition and endemic culture often is an improvement on old or outdated models. While the beauty of the world's diverse array of people is lost, so too are some of the cruel draconian practices.

Think of how fortunate it is that we no longer sacrifice human beings like the ancient Maya did for their gods. Think of the Korowai in New Guinea, modern-day cannibals whose gruesome traditions may not live much longer in the globalized world. Think of the Samburu in Kenya whose ancient traditions normalize child brides and sexual assault.

These examples are counter-pointed by equally brutal reactionaries. The Samburu, for example, suffer heavily at the hands of their own government and Kenyan police forces, victimized callously through beatings, larceny, arson, and rape. Much of this tension is fueled by the tourism industry and government usurping of Samburu lands for national parks. It would seem that neither the Samburu nor the Kenyan authorities act toward each other with progressivism in mind.

Thinking forward it may become more and more necessary to study the diversity of humankind, as it seems the spectrum of culture is ever thinning. While sushi can be obtained in any part of the world, one may encounter as many McDonald's franchises in Japan as they would sushi restaurants. The history of the world shows that beyond a doubt cultures come and go, live and die much the way human beings do. As this process meets the unprecedented rise of globalized exchange, it will yield both great and terrible changes for cultures all around the globe.

Arguably the most that can be done is to catalog the history of these soon-to-be-lost cultures, while providing infrastructure and compassion for the people of Antia, the Awa, and the Samburu.

State Capitalism

The dominant model for our adolescent globalized world is currently state capitalist. Readdressing, the definition used for our purposes is as follows: "State capitalism is a system in which the private entities in possession of the most capital create or enforce policy, precedent, and legislation."

In traditional capitalism it is generally implied that the government and private sector operate independently, so as to deter market monopolies. Contrary to this, state capitalism fuses the private and public sectors to effectively invoke preferential government treatment of select private companies. It is upon this crux that the modern global markets have emerged. In terms of homogenization, culture mustn't be the only concern, but also industry.

Under the Viacom entertainment umbrella is Paramount Pictures, Nickelodeon, Comedy Central, Spike, MTV, CMT, DreamWorks, and much more. Under Nestlé rests L'Oréal shampoos, Wonka candies, Gerber, and Purina dog food, to name a few. Procter and Gamble owns Crest toothpastes, Dawn dish liquid, Tide, Tampax, Gillette razors, Duracell, Vicks, and Ivory soaps.

This extreme dominance of select companies is no coincidence. These large-scale conglomerates are also the frequent recipients of government subsidies, and they are the prime candidates for the lobbying of national governments and submitting former employees for government offices.

By way of manipulating policy, precedents, and the docket of government officials, select private entities can undermine the supposed chief components of traditional capitalism. While globalization has shown definite promise of upward mobility, its ties to state capitalism have disturbing implications.

Broadly speaking, a primary concern with state capitalist influence on national policies is the lack of investment private companies have in sovereign nations. While multinational conglomerates may rely on demand and production from specific countries, many operate in dozens of places across the world. This diversification means that if the US dollar were to fail, if China were to implement a strict EPA-like agency, or if Afghanistan nationalized its mineral reserves, multinationals would not be hindered for very long. They could simply produce and sell in different global markets.

By creating an ambiguous and one-sided relationship between themselves and national governments, a multinational corporation can then use the policies of entire nations as their own privatized assets.

This removal of national autonomies walks a thin line. In one sense a more "flat" set of standards for world policy could assure extremely positive results for the environment or human rights. Yet at the same time a "flat" de-nationalized world is at serious risk for manipulation by the large-scale private sector. This is seen with the wars in Afghanistan over poppy and mineral production, conflicts in Iraq over oil, the housing bubble bailouts in 2008, the early 1900s consolidation of banking in the US, or any of the other previously mentioned private-public sector marriages.

As lobbying becomes increasingly commonplace in global government, the voice of large conglomerates outweighs the voice of constituents in terms of policy. Citizens United is an excellent centerpiece for this point.

With a name bathed in irony, Citizens United is a pro-corporate advocacy group that pushes the United States government to relinquish regulations in regard to campaign finance. Heavily subsidized by the billionaire Koch family, this organization is designed to treat corporate entities as though they were individual people, giving them passage to the inner workings of public government. It is through this medium that biased politics are created through corrupted, faux-representative exchange.

Through the vices of campaign donations, congressional lobbying, and the replacement of true political candidates with former corporate officials, the state capitalist government shrugs off notions of actual democracy. Perpetual wars, industrial subsidies, currency inflation, market homogeneity, and mass incarceration are all side effects of this pseudo-hidden aristocracy.

Manipulation of government in this sense resembles fascism, if only in the meaning that there is a connection between deeply established industrial and public sectors. However, the agenda of the modern state capitalist is veiled far more effectively than Mussolini or Hitler. In particular these older more overt methods of consolidating power would limit secularism and development. This made counterculture easy to establish, as any polarized ideology has a definite binary. It is extremely easy to unify under anti-fascist or anti-communist banners, as proponents of secularism or economic mobility have a defined enemy.

As discussed earlier, antithesis is one of the easiest ways to define identity. This applies both personally and nationally. The major design flaw in authoritarian rule, both left or right aligned, is that in its hardline ideals it helps to define dissident identity. By default, overtly defined power structures create their own antitheses that guarantee countercultural backlash. It is far more difficult to define entrenched power under the guises of free market and democracy, the illusions of which are maintained easily under state capitalism.

With state capitalism, democracy and the free market can exist within margins. Democratic participation is still a reality, though political candidates tend to be limited to a small spectrum of aristocrats and former lobbyists. There is a decentralized market that permits open industry, yet these industries are dominated in near perpetuity by major economic players. These are sterilized versions of democracy and market freedom, just enough to minimize counterculture and derail mass dissidence.

Much in the same strategy as the limited hangout, it is necessary to give away a certain amount of freedom in order to maintain an overall power structure. Authoritarian structures of the past illustrate such a concept with intense clarity. In order to consolidate power and economy on a global scale, it would require keeping a measure of democracy and market freedom open, while rendering systematic preservation of top-down established-determination.

Based on these observations, state capitalism becomes far more extensive than national political systems. Aforementioned political systems can be used as tools by multinational state capitalist structures, much in the same fashion as schismatic operations. Given that overt displays of political rhetoric imply their own antithesis, the idea of fascist parties, communist parties, bipartisanism, liberalism, or conservatism take on a new meaning.

Namely it is implied that polarized themes in national affairs would be encouraged by globalized power structures; the reason being that national strength remains divided and directed away from entrenched international power. This is similar to both Bacon's

Rebellion or the subsidizing of anti-Western propaganda by the House of Saud. So long as the culture and counterculture are at odds domestically, larger systemic power remains intact.

How much of this is intentional? How many complicit parties are engaged in such an idea? How would one nation or individual abstain from involvement that empowers said systems? The answers to these questions are vague. The very nature of such a system defies focus and accurate analysis. What can be considered realistically are deteriorative trends in national sovereignties worldwide. Removal of protective tariffs, neo-imperial use of military power, corporate-drafted trade agreements or market doctrine, and subsidy of toxic businesses all imply a directive made to preserve industrial homogeneity on a global scale.

In many ways it can be surmised that world governments are well aware of these trends. The general complicit reaction to this is likely a means of keeping up with one's neighbors economically, for fear of being left behind in the process of globalization. If there were an effort by a singular nation to buck the trends of state capitalism, they would undoubtedly be at a severe economic and civil disadvantage. Without the same means to accommodate modernized technology, infrastructure, necessities, or entertainment this hypothetical nation would suffer greatly in comparison to its complicit counterparts. Furthermore, multinational state capitalist companies wouldn't suffer at all, or at least very slightly.

One of two scenarios could play out:

1. The previously discussed migration of production and sales from global companies to different markets. If the United States were to somehow eliminate its demand for foreign goods, large Western conglomerates could still pursue

aggressive sales strategies in Asia, South America, Europe, or Canada. Through redirection of supply and acquisition of smaller regional companies, the loss of one nation's clientele is a mere setback to large-scale globalist industry.

2. The use of political influence by state capitalist entities to incite war against non-compliant nations. Be it the Central American and Caribbean conquests documented by Smedley Butler, the removal of prospective African independence via Libya, or the undermining of Iranian self-determination through operations such as Ajax, many full-scale military engagements are often designed to consolidate economy and global power.

Many questions arise from the ever-connected globalized version of state capitalism. Perhaps this consolidated power and undermining of nationalities is only temporary. Perhaps to establish the sheer scale of worldwide commerce we require there must be firmly directed capital and a concentrated agenda. Yet even if this logic operates accurately, where and when does the paradigm cease? Can the entities in power be trusted to disperse when it is finally appropriate? Do many of them even know or understand their role on the current stage?

Or alternatively: Is there even altruistic purpose to this power consolidation? Could it be the remnants of industrial revolutions past, diversifying and clawing their way through new markets in an effort to retain relevance in an ever-expanding world economy?

Most questions so large probably have many answers. Given that these musings affect billions of people across the world, there may be truth in each answer. A binary response only serves to polarize, simplify, and depreciate the content of the subject matter.

Notes

Subjects of concern for globalization are extremely difficult to navigate. Perhaps one of the most troubling is that of cultural loss and dilution. This is truly one of the most double-edged to discuss, as there are two powerful human limitations working to shape opinion.

One is the ever-recurring hurdle of moral debt. When it is understood that a culture will be lost, there is a ping of human empathy that accompanies it. For cultural integrity to be lost, a piece of the human experience is lost as well. The trials and tribulations, successes and failures, arts and folklore, villains and heroes of an entire people will be scattered to the wind; perhaps only to exist through a few brief sentences in someone's book. The feeling of this loss can cross any social barriers. The irony of it is powerful, to say the least.

An individual in the West may sit in a Starbucks to enjoy a cup of coffee, and experience these feelings, without batting an eye at the source of their drink. Many coffee giants operate using standards set in third-world nations by Conservation International—whose many clients include Exxon, Walmart, Monsanto, Shell, and Chevron, to name a few. Such names don't exactly scream notoriety for the preservation of culture. Suffice to say their involvement in the third-world and global community hinges on a profit margin basis.

For all the concern in the developed world for preserving cultural identity, the demand for modern products undermines much of the recourse for said preservation. For a major company the bottom line is to make money and remain relevant. Therefore, any momentum toward cultural accountability must be initiated by the consumer.

Without detracting from the importance of preservation, the counterpoint to this would be that cultures have risen and fallen throughout history. The loss of human culture is as predictable as changes in societal structure, political or moral standards, and an end to life itself.

It still feels incredibly sour to allow homogenization and lust for modernization to ruin the beautiful incarnations of humanity, and for that matter, nature. The globalized economy and increased demand for products have an extremely detrimental effect on the earth. Carbon emissions, mass farming, and the loss of the rainforest or other climates contribute to this profoundly negative imprint.

A separate limitation exists through the human ego. For many developed nations there is little to fear in terms of cultural loss, relative to the remaining indigenous peoples of the world. Yet a constant fear looms for many that secularism will intrude upon culture and ethnic relevance. For nations that are experiencing a mass influx of individuals of different colors and creeds, there can be heavy dissent from long-standing social groups. The fear of lessened economic or political importance, intermarriages, and dilution of the long-standing culture serves as a conduit for fear—and eventually hatred.

Culture as a whole can be heavily burdened by ego. As the world grows in terms of secularity, increased diversity will change national identities. This will in turn prompt measures of backlash from cultures that were formerly dominant. Even if these cultures are in no danger of dying out, they will in many cases react unfavorably to widening secular margins due to insecurity with a change in status quo. This insecurity is tied to the basic human function of ego, an identification of self that is meant to aid in survival. Cultural subsets that aren't in jeopardy may therefore still react to secularism as if they were in danger of extinction, manifesting in forms of racism, nationalism, sexism, and xenophobia.

The final note for these sections reiterates the indescribable impact of globalization upon environment. Demand for even the most basic products has devastating ramifications for the global ecology, and its unsustainable nature is hardly addressed by the prevalent power systems in place.

Something so trivial as a nondescript white T-shirt requires nearly seven hundred gallons of water to create, a considerable amount of pollutive fertilizer and pesticides, large amounts of electrical power, as well as manual labor from third-world workshops. For the creation of every new product and the continuation of every entrenched industry there is a cost, not just in terms of liquidity, but also in terms of sustainability. The ultimate goal of globalization will require focus on successful and sustainable models, should it be expected to continue well into the future.

Prospects

Whether we and our politicians know it or not Nature is party to all our deals and decisions, and she has more votes, a longer memory, and a sterner sense of justice than we do.
—Wendell Berry

Many people believe that decentralization means loss of control. That's simply not true. You can improve control if you look at control as the control of events and not people. Then, the more people you have controlling events—the more people you have that care about controlling the events, the more people you have proactively working to create favorable events—the more control you have within the organization, by definition.
—Wilbur L Creech

The atomic bomb made the prospect of future war unendurable. It has led us up those last few steps to the mountain pass; and beyond there is a different country.
—J. Robert Oppenheimer

The prospect of success in achieving our most cherished dream is not without its terrors. Who is more deprived and alone than the man who has achieved his dream?
—Brendan Behan

If you assume that there is no hope, you guarantee that there will be no hope. If you assume that there is an instinct for freedom, that there are opportunities to change things, then there is a possibility that you can

contribute to making a better world.
—Noam Chomsky

You cannot hope to build a better world without improving the individuals. To that end, each of us must work for his own improvement and, at the same time, share a general responsibility for all humanity, our particular duty being to aid those to whom we think we can be most useful.
—Marie Curie

Our human compassion binds us the one to the other—not in pity or patronizingly, but as human beings who have learnt how to turn our common suffering into hope for the future.
—Nelson Mandela

We have also arranged things so that almost no one understands science and technology. This is a prescription for disaster. We might get away with it for a while, but sooner or later this combustible mixture of ignorance and power is going to blow up in our faces.
—Carl Sagan

Analysis of politics, the humanities, and sociology is no longer confined to an intellectual elite, nor the respective institutions for education in such matters. For the first time in history knowledge of the arts and sciences can be learned on a global scale by anyone who is interested. Additionally, individuals can contribute in new and unprecedented ways to the great zeitgeist. Modern social constructs lie upon a precipice of change, new and tenacious.

It is reminiscent of the early twentieth century when old and outdated monarchies began to fall, being replaced by new and revolutionary political experiments. The internet, cryptocurrencies, and consumer democracy have the potential to shed the entrenched power that has existed since the inception of the most recent industrial revolutions.

It would not be an exaggeration to consider that such dramatic changes could offer new forms of political and social movement.

For each section of this book there is a reiteration that binaries rarely exist, if ever, in politics or sociology. By keeping the etymology of social dialogue open, critical thought is increasingly necessary to express the views and needs of individuals. This also provides a way to articulate the vast, bright world of possibilities and prospects for the future. In this sense, the upward mobility promised by the inevitable trends in globalism can be realized firstly through heightened consciousness and rejection of binaries.

While facets of entrenched power may be guided toward reformation, they will not enact said reformation themselves. Reforming governmental and social models has proven to be no easy task. Secularism, the free market, and higher expectations for upward mobility only intensify the strain in demand for massive reforms on a global scale.

Implementation of such hefty demands would no doubt be a grueling battle, but it seems on many levels that the gears are already in motion. It will be central for these changes to note that entrenched power exists in forms above the individuals that comprise its structure. It would also be imperative to provide new means of economy for those displaced from defunct monopolies in the future.

If the fuel and electric industry were to abandon coal, coal miners and industry officials would still need work. Providing ingress to the market of solar and renewable energy to these professionals would prevent social backlash and assist in power de-consolidation.

Each market monopoly has such a reality to be considered if progressivism is to be achieved. The future is flush with prospects, should the proper action be taken to attain them.

De-Centralization of Power

There was an ultimate reason behind the first democracies in Greece. The centralization of power in government had become all too obvious for the average Grecian to abide, and the status of political aristocrats was questioned heavily by the people.

In so many words there was a majority feeling that power was too consolidated amongst the social elite, religious officials, the military, and so on. The ability to vote would theoretically provide some measure of presence in government from the proletariat, thereby removing the monopoly over Grecian power and economics.

The same sentiment could be likened to various workers' movements and revolutions throughout history; the idea being that power could be usurped from entrenched constructs. It would seem that the longer mankind exists, the most natural evolution for civilization and government is to strive to become more liberated in our societies. The initial purpose behind this was likely to provide a better life quality for more individuals, by taking resources from the elite and redistributing them to the masses.

While this goal remains the same for much of the developing world, major nations such as the USA have begun to experience a sense of static as to what clear power reform would be.

Political reform is enacted to meet necessity. When necessity-based needs are met, a society seeks entertainment. When needs for entertainment are met, there is potential for stagnation in terms of political evolution. The people do not aim to analyze entrenched power as consciously as they may if masses were bored, hungry, or jobless. This is not to say that poverty or civil issues do not exist in developed nations. Instead this illustrates that a unified and intellectual means of political recourse is harder to achieve when the citizenry is splintered between surplus and deficit, affluence and poverty. In and of itself large-scale capitalist systems provide their own schismatic operations by way of extreme class divide.

What is truly interesting is the counterpoint to capitalism's divisive nature. While it creates implied schisms in the populace, it can also present a multitude of ways to alter power structures.

One of the most intriguing prospects of the twenty-first century relates back to liquidity and its effect on the foundations of civilized society. In 2009 a man under the pseudonym Satoshi Nakamoto created the first all-digital currency. Unlike its fiat brothers that were in the market, its digital nature would not mean that it was de-standardized. It would have a finite amount, being divisible up to a significant decimal point. In this way Nakamoto's design would ensure currency worth without threat of hyperinflation, while also providing potential for the currency to fluctuate in value as per its market demand.

The most defining quality of this new currency would ultimately be its ability to decentralize both monopolies of power and liquidity.

Bitcoin and other cryptocurrencies (Litecoin, Ethereum, Neo, Dash, or Monero) are not distributed or controlled by governmental institutions. Each of these liquid assets operate without government monopoly to contain them, surpassing long-standing national and societal precedents regarding the nature of money. The centralization of capital, the production of capital, and the policy of loans or liquid exchange are all ways in which entrenched power can thrive.

Countless national economies have been usurped from under their respective constituents through monopolies of currency. By removing the middleman of national government from currency exchange, there is a re-democratization of liquidity, similar to pre-Federal Reserve banking and currency markets. However to fully follow such a comparison, the volatility of these markets has yet to be fully seen.

If true independent competition is established for currencies, it could become necessary for world governments to be more accountable for their own fiscal actions. To invest in a cryptocurrency one no longer needs to also invest in a country. They can gain decentralized assets with total removal from entrenched power. It can also be reasoned that while Bitcoin currently dominates the market, the cryptocurrency model will improve over time and diversify.

In terms of accountability, Bitcoin's founding anonymity has been a source of concern. Without a product figurehead, there has been considerable market speculation, but that hasn't stopped a rise in Bitcoin's value, from $.08 in July 2010 to over $15,000 in January of 2018.

It must be re-emphasized that the sheer impact of liquidity upon a society can make, break, or shape an entire civilization. What the creation of cryptocurrency shows is that society on a global level is searching for new and evolved means of liquidity. It is likely the emergence of Bitcoin in 2009 may have been a reactionary response to the market crash of 2008, wherein state capitalist institutions made billions off of subprime loans and derivative sales of the accumulated debt. Banking and loan personnel made immense amounts off of commissions and allowed their own businesses to go bankrupt, knowing that bailouts would be supplied in US dollars.

The entire world economy came to a screeching halt for several minutes due to these irresponsible malpractices, prompting a need in the free market for alternatives to state-sanctioned currencies.

The practice of power consolidation is also becoming more limited due to a symbiotic relationship between the public forum and security. The need for security has often been a crutch for entrenched power to grow, through the means of fear and identity development. The true needs for security have been difficult to discern from the manipulation of fear by entrenched power structures. However, the mass influx of information made possible by the internet has created an average citizen with extreme potential for critical thought.

For every homogenized narrative of events there are hundreds of counter narratives, allowing individuals the opportunity to use their own judgment in affairs rather than relying on the limited margins of state bias. As the largest public forum in history, the internet is doing its rightful job in supplying meaningful dialogue for the purposes of social evolution.

Mounting secularization is also creating cracks in the bedrock of long-standing entrenched power. Religious, ethnic, and racial dominance in major nations across the world is becoming a thing of the past. This may be happening at a slower pace in some parts of the world than in others, but the reality is quite clear that secularity is on the perpetual rise.

For the West this means a lessened emphasis on Christian-leaning social policy and doctrine. For the Middle East it implies eventual trending away from traditional monarchies like the House of Saud to a parliamentary system like that of the United Kingdom. Globally, it will demand a further empowerment of the average constituent, worker, and proletariat. The list of implications can easily go on.

A widening secular population doesn't just mean more diversity of people in politics and positions of power. It is indicative of a widening social consciousness. In particular it encourages more coverage of demographics in education, awareness, and understanding. Should Muslim children be more present in the school systems of the United States, there can be more visibility into the history and culture of Islam as a whole. The same can be said for most any group of secular citizens anywhere in the world. Should the content of citizenry change, so too will the content of a nation's collective understanding of the world in its entirety.

Without the presence of schismatic operations, secularism has great promise to bring unity and remove prejudices. Alternatively it can be used as a Trojan Horse, geared toward boons for multinational entities. The Middle East has provided a unique study in such secular movement.

In Syria, for example, power has long been monopolized by a subset of Shia Islam called Alawite. There is a difference between Alawite and traditional Islam. Many of the followers find unique distinction in their geological origin and triad interpretation of a monotheistic god. Though Syria has been run by Alawites since the 1970s its population has been primarily secular, governed by Socialist Baathism. Unlike in Saudi Arabia, there was no specific state-sponsored religion for the populace, yet the Alawites held much of the power in politics, as well as in the Syrian Army.

Given this disparity there was quite a bit of dissent in Syria amongst marginalized groups, particularly Sunni Muslims and some Shia sects. These dissenting masses also held in their ranks several forms of extremism, which were viewed as a built-in stay-behind by international coalitions. It would prove obvious to any world power that overthrowing the Syrian regime could be done by arming extremist factions and using dissent against the Alawites to their advantage.

The Syrian Civil War that began in 2011 was just such a conflict. Though Syria was secular it still had aristocratic undertones that were a chink in its armor, an Achilles' heel that would ultimately be utilized by nations like the United States to dismantle the Alawite government. The purpose of this would conceivably be to pave the way for multinational businesses and neoliberal trade, much in the style of Smedley Butler's accounts in Central America, the Far East, and the Caribbean.

Once more it can't be emphasized enough that these considerations are not meant to polarize the United States, Alawites, or extremism. Recounting these events only serves to illustrate cause and effect in geopolitics while shedding light to their function.

On the whole it has been secularism that has made the great advances in human history. From the Silk Road, to the trade-savvy Phoenicians, to the blend of cultures in the Rus, it is continually illustrated that secular ideas help to construct the foundations of society on a global scale.

Global Community and National Power

Secularization extends well beyond the scope of individual definition. As the world becomes more connected there must also be a secularized balance of power between the aims of the international community and individual nations.

Should the international community impose overzealous regulations that impact national sovereignty, there will be homogenized power and likely aristocratic despotism. Should individual nations disregard international dialogue they put themselves at risk of falling behind in development, economy, and social progress. The two forces must balance each other in order to provide a feasible environment for social and political evolution.

The effect of state capitalism on these two forces is detrimental, to say the least. Constructive action is difficult to achieve when the global community or national powers are being used to further privatized gain, each being used to undermine the other where applicable.

This is done through a combination of lobbying, placement of ex-corporate officials into political power, and industry-drafted legislation. In the case of the IMF and World Bank, there is an international monopoly on development loans. These institutions are the primary source for developing nations to acquire monetary loans, offering credit at interest to the third world. Yet the IMF and WB reserves are backed by the currencies of sovereign nations. What does this mean?

For a moment let's make this into a more concise analogy:

Two friends are conversing at a local pub. One man is a contractor, specializing in home construction, where his business leads the market. The other is a venture capitalist who borrows money from others, invests, sells at a profit, and returns what he initially borrowed.

Over a few drinks they speak of two subjects. One is that they recently became aware of a third man who has moved to town and that he is in desperate need of a house, but has no money. The second is that many investors wish to help the man out with a loan at interest, but our venture capitalist wants to beat them to the punch.

The contractor has an old associate who used to work with him and recently became mayor of the town. He says to the venture capitalist that he will speak with his old associate and petition to make other lenders illegal in their city. In exchange the venture capitalist will make himself available for low-interest loans to the contractor. The idea works as planned, and for a cut of the profits the mayor enacts an order that only allows our venture capitalist to make loans.

Now enter the third man. He is new to town and needs to have a house built. He has no money, but is told that he may take a loan from the town's venture capitalist to build his house (at interest, of course). He does so and hires our contractor to build his home. The contractor gives a cut of his pay to the mayor for helping the two achieve their plan (this is lobbying), and the venture capitalist will collect money from the third man until his debt is paid.

The debt, however, will increase due to interest, which frequently compounds to exponential amounts. Perhaps the third man will never be able to pay with money, so he must have his paycheck garnished or sell some of his own property.

In this analogy the contractor is the major development industry, the venture capitalist is the dominant monetary system, the mayor represents complicit national governments, and the third man is the developing world. Development industry and monetary systems operate on international levels, while using influence over national governments to further their objectives. One of these objectives is the neocolonial subjugation of the developing world. Doing so underpays third-world nations for their massive input of resources, goods, labor, and GDP.

This is to say that a shirt company in Bangladesh pays its tailor twenty-five cents per sale, is sold by the Bangladeshi assembly house for a dollar, and is sold again by a major Western company for thirty dollars. Such a design is true for many products, from precious metals to edible produce. Homogenizing the market of loans to the developing world creates a stranglehold on upward mobility for the people in these countries. Our third man will take whatever underpaid work he can get to feed his family, try to pay off his loans, and keep his house in the "town" of global commerce.

Keep in mind: In both the analogy and in actual practice loan money from the venture capitalist never actually goes to the third man. It travels directly to major industry, leaving out any sort of personal or preferential monetary needs for development in the third world.

Suppose a small and underdeveloped country is in desperate need of clean water; a loan from the IMF or World Bank will likely be funneled directly to oil conglomerates or major agricultural companies rather than to waterworks. The foundations needed for societal function are overlooked in lieu of industrial prerequisites, amounting to not only a perpetuation of failed policy, but also a destructive behavior that endangers countless individuals. This becomes immensely destructive in the face of an emergency.

In 2017 Hurricane Irma decimated the US territory of Puerto Rico, a small cluster of islands that were considering either independent statehood or becoming a formal addition to the United States.

Infrastructure for the province was utterly destroyed, leaving countless families without power or running water. Buildings, disaster relief organizations, food or medicine outlets, and much more were rendered functionally useless. Though international relief was needed desperately, Puerto Rico owed large debts to Wall Street and associated companies, and thus was unable to purchase or afford the help they would need. Instead of extending assistance to Puerto Ricans in their time of need, the question from the financial and development community would be (paraphrasing): "How will they pay for this?" or, "They already owe a lot of money."

While Puerto Rico has been the beneficiary of many World Bank and IMF initiatives, it has been unable to funnel these resources into proper developmental avenues. The primary function of its dealings with the World Bank and IMF has traditionally been to provide context for corporate businesses to operate smoothly in Puerto Rico, leaving the average citizen in economic and risk-related purgatory.

This situation is a staple of the developing world and a recurring theme that hinders these nations from rising in the international hierarchy. The use of debt peonage from predefined sources is able to keep small nations down economically, socially, and developmentally. Even in the contingency of disaster there is little reprieve from debt. In terms of market speculation, it is reasonable to consider that if small countries were able to take full profit margin advantage of their exports they could be more self-sufficient in times of disaster or instability. Debts accrued through development loans could also be repaid more comfortably in such a scenario.

However, if this were the reality it would remove power from multinational cabals. Heightened national power detracts from the ability for non-national powers to influence domestic governments, biting into multinational profit margins as well as currency monopolies. In this sense, allowing the international community to dictate parameters for loans issued to the third world is akin to letting a wolf run a butcher shop.

If the described empowerment were achievable in the developing world what could possibly happen? If national governments in Africa, South America, and South Asia were to become empowered like Western governments are, how would it reshape the global community?

Strides toward actual independence for the developing world have the potential to deconstruct and restructure long-standing hierarchies that have existed since the last industrial revolution, or even prior. As globalization has been led primarily by developed Western nations, there is a prevalence in policy that favors a select few world contenders. Large countries such as China have been able to adapt more easily to the "flat" world than Uganda, for example, but even the superpower of the East has incredible levels of income disparity and third-world conditions.

To realize the potential of globalization on democracy and upward mobility, the third world is of utmost priority in terms of development. If progressivism is limited in the developing world by entrenched power, it ultimately contradicts the ideology of capitalist socio-economics—namely that market freedom should provide a fairer footing for industries, social mobility, and individualism.

National power is necessary to maintain in order to check and balance multinational entities. Yet at the same time there must be a means of monitoring national climates and their interaction with the global community. It is for this reason that organizations like the United Nations are advertised to exist, as well as NGOs of many kinds. Setting standards for the global community is of increasing importance as secularism grows. For a globalized community to interact smoothly there must be a standard of minimal conduct for ethics, trade, finance, environment, and communication. Without these being established there is danger of economic crisis, genocide, or war.

The role of international oversight can't be understated as the world becomes more closely connected.

The central idea of democracy is focused on a system of checks and balances, between governmental branches and constituent representation. To generate upward mobility and self-determination on a global scale we must discuss how to implement checks and balances between the global community and national power. Without autonomy a nation ceases to have the identity or ability to prevent international monopoly. Without international oversight a nation may not be able to keep up with global standards.

Either of these realities can manifest in power consolidation, or breakdown of the four societal foundations.

If the purpose of society and group civilization is to improve the collective quality of life, that goal must be addressed and kept in mind during the process of global unity that is underway. A loss of this understanding has destructive prospects that are truly unprecedented.

National Power and Individual Determination

Before election time in the United States there is a flurry of activity. Amongst the prevailing Democratic and Republican parties there is movement to redraw district lines within the United States, for the purposes of misrepresenting the popular vote and controlling voter outcome.

Let's pretend that in a fictional state there are 40 percent Democrats and 60 percent Republicans. Elections are decided by the number of districts won, so if either party wins a majority of districts, they win the political position.

Now let's also say that there are Democrats in charge before an election. Before the election begins they are able to redraw district lines to show four Democratic districts versus two Republican ones. Despite the 60 percent per capita Republican vote, district line manipulation designates the Democrats as winners.

This practice is known commonly as *gerrymandering* and is used by both political parties in the United States as one of many ways that modern democracy is undermined. Lobbying, of course, has similar implications, as does corporate campaign finance. These three methods consolidate the docket of both legislation and potential representatives.

Should a large state capitalist company wish to enact some sort of governmental policy, they can do so by directly pressuring elected representatives. This is done by dually financing the aforementioned representatives during their campaign and creating a quid-pro-quo relationship through lobbying. Given that better campaign finance yields a more successful candidate, the reality becomes such that politics require corporate backing simply to compete for representative seats.

In a not so subtle stroke of irony the three practices discussed remove significant quantities of "representation" and replace them with sterile, uniform corporate doctrine. The will of the constituents is hardly a match for state capitalist influence as it pervades the legislature, the executive branch, the media, the military, education, development, and finance. Initiatives like Citizens United dictate consideration that corporations can act as individuals and inject their voice into government policy. The major pitfall of this is that the voice of a large-scale company and an average individual are not heard at the same volume.

If a large conglomerate is able to finance the campaign of a successful elected representative, there is a precedent that said representative will work toward the aims of their financier rather than those of the average voter. Should the two have differing needs or wants, the larger monetary influence is likely to prevail.

This analysis may seem dismissive, but it is of the utmost necessity for the forward development of government, as well as political evolution into the twenty-first century. While national and global powers require balance, so too do the wills of national government and individual constituents. If standards for democratic process are not established and sought to be improved upon there will only be pseudo-democratic policy, wherein one may choose their brand of soft drink but not the use of their tax dollars. Such standards must be demanded by constituents of their respective national governments.

With some element of conjecture, it is with critique and abstinence from misleading political process that these aims may be achieved. Praising and participating in dysfunctional political manifestations is, in essence, to be a part of their perpetuation.

The power of the individual is undeniably set to increase as globalization continues to make strides. New industries will yield vast job markets, new currencies will strip liquidity monopolies of their power, old industries will be improved upon, and technology will enhance education to a new and unprecedented level. These are all realities that are being seen daily in the twenty-first century. Part of this driving force is the inevitable human want for self-determination. Even individuals that are directly part of an established power structure will invest in markets and motives outside of their control, if they deem them to be profitable. By doing so systemic power shoots itself in the foot, while making profit along the way.

Cryptocurrencies are once again a prime example, removing monopolies from the world of liquidity and exchange. If these mediums were to gain immense foothold in global finance, they could threaten dominant national currencies. Yet Wall Street, credit card companies, and large-scale business are all making moves to accept and invest in blockchain currency technology.

Despite their position of power and control over market homogeneity, these entities are investing in the future to stay relevant. This shows very well that large-scale power structures are not static, they are full of moving components and individuals. It is because of this reality that developmental progress is a societal inevitability.

If one facet of entrenched power invests in outlying developmental growth it will cause others to follow, operating in the same herd mannerisms that control market statistics around the world. Imagining global monopolies as a single unified force misrepresents the actuality that these groups are, though still working closely with one another, splintered.

It will prove to be through these opportunities in market diversity that individuals will increase their presence in political evolution. A single individual may have the key to drive their ideas into a market just as effectively as a multinational corporation, removing monopolization as they do so.

Through crowdfunding, social media marketing, 3D printing, digital cloud storage, public domain patent release, and forward-thinking means of finance or exchange, there are countless ways in which the "flat" earth can be revolutionized in positive and non-exclusive ways.

While entrenched power may invest in new development it will also push back. As the current paradigm of power is constructed of moving autonomous parts, each part will act differently to this shifting landscape. While Company A may invest in cryptocurrency, Company B may work toward lobbying the government to make cryptocurrencies illegal. This is where the balance of power between national government and individuals becomes so important. Should forward-thinking development be hindered by national governments, particularly those in the developed world, it will yield despotism and an unsustainable future for humanity as a whole.

The destructive nature of entrenched power through state capitalism isn't a model that can be sustained environmentally, or from an ethical perspective. It becomes the most important responsibility for individuals in a democracy to remove self-serving special interests from the decisions of government, whose core function is to provide for constituents as a whole.

A significant part of individual controls upon government is a unified social understanding. For this to happen individuals do not need to agree upon a set limitation of political beliefs or margins; instead they only need to agree upon the demand that the government serves them and not vice versa. Promoting and encouraging secularity is a paramount means to this, as is a standard of education that has better emphasis on societal foundations and political structures.

It is the intrinsic nature of humanity to be curious and innovative, especially in the spectrum of civilized development.

From the development of chemical combustion and compasses in Asia, the studies of cymatics or geometries in the Mediterranean, the establishment of algorithmic mathematics in the Middle East, the musical polyrhythms and surgical strides made in Africa, or the advances in modern medicine from Europe, there is a united truth that human existence serves to enhance itself through the means of all people and ethnicities. Quite literally the only preventative hold upon these developments has come from schismatic issues of government or dogma associated with entrenched power. These dogmas can be religious, ethnic, moral, or fear based.

To enjoy modern life in the developed world and fail to attribute it to an immense plethora of peoples is fallacy, a blinded instance of missing the forest for the trees. Such exclusive beliefs only serve to perpetuate stagnant political despotism and homogeneity. To empower individuals and provide the power checks that national governments need, individuals must be able to empower each other first and foremost by removing the yoke of schisms.

Notes

A trilateral balance of powers will be the determining factor for the future of human civilization. If individuals can check national government, national government can check international coalitions and industry. If international coalitions and industry can provide standards for national governments, national governments can in turn provide better infrastructure and contingency plans for individuals. If left to their own devices each of these three will resort to motives of special interest, preventing upward mobility.

As society divides and diversifies it is often hard to keep in mind the initial goal of social structuring, much less the importance and condition of its foundations. Increased emphasis on self-determination can also serve as a blinder for many people, consuming everyday thought with personal growth rather than consideration for society as a whole. This prevents macro-analysis of social settings. As with all things, these two outlooks require balance. A society policed by its populace will ultimately ensure a wider margin of self-determination. However, that same self-determination has the ability to blind a populace from policing its society.

In a strange catch-22 there is a balance of social macro-awareness and personal gratification to be had if a civilization aims for true progress. It will be by taking personal initiatives, revitalizing education, and seeking uniformity through balances of power that the world will shift into its next great phase. It is without question that this transformation is already underway. The only remaining thing to be considered is this:

How will you be a part of it?

Acknowledgements

I would like to thank my parents first and foremost for their unwavering support in all my endeavors. They have both worked hard to mold me and everyone around them into independent thinkers, whose hopes are high and hearts free of hate. I would like to thank my wonderful wife, Blayne, for always believing in me even when I have not, whose words and confidence are the greatest gifts I could ever receive. To my closest friends, I thank you for you sharing conversation with me over a beer or some coffee, for aiding in the formation of my outlooks and giving me perspectives I would not have on my own.

I would also like to give recognition to the society I live in, where I may voice my opinions and ideas freely. I do not take it for granted that I may write this book with no fear of persecution, that I may share my experience in the hopes that others may find it valuable.

While many people may not have the same liberty I do, it is my sincere desire that we may all become equal parts of this world.

With thanks,

Jaron

Bibliography Available At:

https://jaronpearlman.com/iconoclasm-bibliography